"Mike Ricksecker has broken new ground with A Walk in the Shadows, illuminating a rather cryptic element of paranormal activity which has endured decades of speculation and skepticism, providing more curiosity than clarity. The author sheds new light on the subject with his erudite commentary and insightful treatment of the anomaly, offering a fresh perspective regarding the existence and origin of shadow people. Known as an exceptional writer in the field of supernatural research, Mike translates his thoughts to the written word with ease and grace. As his personal history unfolds by the page, experiences which have transpired over the course of his lifetime serve to inform, providing the ultimate template for what eventually becomes implausible deniability. I believe every word of it because I've lived it. Dare to delve in. He will gently guide you through this authentic and enormously valuable contribution to the cause of human enlightenment."

– Andrea Perron, Best-selling author, *House Of Darkness House Of Light*

Other Books by Mike Ricksecker:

Campfire Tales: Midwest

Ghostorian Case Files: Volume 1

Ghosts and Legends of Oklahoma

Ghosts of Maryland

System of the Dead

Deadly Heirs

Encounters With The Paranormal: Vol. 1-4

A WALK IN THE SHADOWS

SECOND EDITION

MIKE RICKSECKER

Illustrated by Adam D. Tillery

Second Edition:
First printing

Original artwork by: Adam D. Tillery

Photography by:
Mike Ricksecker
Carl Johnson
Julie Griffin
Cathy E. Gasch

PUBLISHED BY HAUNTED ROAD MEDIA, LLC
www.hauntedroadmedia.com

United States of America

To Mom:
For not thinking your son is nuts.

And to Ron:
We're wide awake … yet sleeping. You may find some of this to be a bit of a Pandora's Box.

Acknowledgments

This project has taken longer than my average time for writing a book, but it has been a passion, and along the journey that passion was aided by so many wonderful people. If I've forgotten anyone in this list, it is certainly not intentional.

I absolutely need to thank Carl Johnson for all of his input and insight into this work. I consulted him several times throughout this process, tapping into his vast reservoir of information and experiences. His twin brother, Keith, and Keith's wife, Sandra, provided some important input as well, and I also have to thank Elise Giammarco Carlson for helping to coordinate and facilitate the passing along of the photographs from Carl contained herein.

There are so many people who contributed stories and provided input, that I am simply going to list them all here and give one immensely large "thank you" to them all. Your stories help provide understanding to others in this world who have had or are having similar experiences. These contributors include (in order of appearance): Shana Wankel, Shawn Gilmore, Tonia Sargisian, Cory Davenport, Michelle LeBaron, Tammy Hayn, Tonya Hayn, Cat Gasch, Lacye Lembke, Cory and Jennifer Heinzen, LulyTubee, Meghan Talbert, Eric Girard, Rob Gutro, Brittney Crabb, Sierra Huber, Dawn Francisco, Elina Ovcharova, and James Annitto.

Helping in this process was the fact that I was able to speak about this topic at a number of conferences over the past few years, which not only kept my mind on the source material for this work, but I also received a ton of feedback and shared experiences from the audience participants who approached me after. I can't possibly track down all the events in which I spoke about shadow people, but some of the notables I'd like to thank are Ken DeCosta who organizes Ocean State ParaCon, Kelly McCarville who runs the Psychic and Paranormal Expo circuit in Iowa, Adrian and Tina Scalf who got me involved with the Arkansas Paranormal Expo, Greg Feketik who puts together Ohio's ParaPsyCon, Robbin Terry who holds the annual AshBash at haunted Ashmore Estates, and most recently as of this writing, Matt Rosvally and Guil Calveria who asked me to speak about shadow people at the 2019 Shockfest Film Festival at which Haunted Road Media won the award for Excellent Media in the Paranormal Field. I also need to recognize Margaret Ehrlich of Inspired Ghost Tracking who has asked me to speak several times at her IGT meetings (and I apologize for not doing more since I moved away from Maryland), and at one of these I gave my very first rough shadow person presentation years ago at which Rob Gutro shared his story that is in this book and really caused me to start looking at shadow entities on a much deeper level.

I would be remiss not to mention all the Mad Hatters of Haunted Road Media's *The Edge Of The Rabbit Hole* livestream show and my amazing co-hostess, Victoria Mundae, who have always been such an immense support and have had to bear through me talking about the "upcoming shadow person book" for the past two years. There are far, far too many people to list here, but I will at least list those who are amongst our "Deep Down The Rabbit Hole" Patreon patrons: Tom McNicholas, beat3airspace, Zippy Davis, Pamela Queen, Jo Chandler, Andrew Cox, Dustin Sommerio, and David Yeisley. All of you, the rest of the Patreon patrons, and all those who watch our content are there with us on a nearly daily basis. You are all amazing!

One other who watches our content all the time and has contributed heavily to this book is Adam Tillery. His amazing artwork graces yet another Haunted Road Media tome, and I'm still floored with the accuracy of his work in capturing exactly how things looked even though he wasn't there. I hope you all enjoy his completely inspired illustrations. Thank you again, Adam!

I also want to thank Dave and Donna Nunnally who run the It's Raining Zen shop (and Indigo Moon and Mississippi Hippie) at the old Mineral Springs Hotel in Alton, Illinois. While Mineral Springs has a nice feature in this book, the friendship of Dave and Donna has always been amazingly supportive, which is far more important. If you're ever in the Alton area, you must stop in at It's Raining Zen … it truly is like family there.

If you haven't yet read Andrea Perron's *House Of Darkness House Of Light* trilogy you need to do so. While I had already had many of my significant shadow people experiences and had already been developing a number of concepts on space and time, reading Andrea's trilogy helped to really flesh out those concepts as I began to see the universe differently through her eyes and the lens of the haunted farmhouse in Harrisville, Rhode Island. It was truly illuminating and transformative. Thank you, Andrea, for everything!

I really do need to thank my mom, Gail Ricksecker, and not just because it's a good thing for a son to thank his mother at times like the publication of a book (after all, she's always been supportive of my writing), but when I was 13 she didn't call me crazy for the shadow entity I saw on several occasions in the house we moved into in Wooster, Ohio. She retained an open mind and affirmed for me what I had seen. It sounds like a small thing, but it was huge.

I also want to thank all of those who have helped with the upcoming *Shadow Dimension* project, which include a few of the aforementioned, such as Carl Johnson, Keith and Sandra Johnson,

Elise Giammarco Carlson, Andrea Perron, and Dave and Donna Nunnally of It's Raining Zen. Also helping in this docu-series which dives deeper into the world of shadows than this book and visits locations with known shadow activity include Mark Anthony, Sam Baltrusis, Jonny Enoch, Corey Heinzen, Mary Marshall, Victoria Mundae, and Coyote Chris Sutton.

Also, a very special thanks to Nicole Guillaume who has helped so much in expanding my vision on how to present this material and research to you, the reader, and the viewers of all the online and television media.

And to the rest, you are immensely appreciated!

Table of Contents

Part IV: Darker Than Dark

Illustrations By Adam D. Tillery:

INTRODUCTION TO THE SECOND EDITION

In the introduction to the first edition of this book, I stated, "Consider this a living document, one that is going to be continuously updated," but I never thought I'd release a second edition so soon after the first. Since the January 2020 release of *A Walk In The Shadows*, my expanding research into this phenomena has taken some extremely interesting twists and turns, especially in the midst of a global pandemic that altered all of my plans for the year. The additional time at home has given me more of an opportunity to hit the books and dive even deeper into what shadow entities may be, and I've been able to have in-depth conversations with a vast number of others in the field to really expand upon this topic. Some of that information you'll find in this second edition, some of it you'll find in the new docu-series *The Shadow Dimension*, and some of it you'll find in one of my next books, titled *Connecting The Universe*. Those that read the first edition will recall I referenced the term "shadow dimension" in the Final Thoughts section which was my intentional hint as to where I'm headed with much of this research.

I also held an online workshop in October 2020, "Unveiling The Shadows," which I'm expanding and turning into an entire online course, including a variety of other courses and an entire community for, what I call, the Connected Universe. That's another intentional hint as to where we're headed.

All of this additional work has led to new and updated content that needed to be included in this work and now has been. This is an ever-growing area of research that has really taken on a life of its own and has led us down new pathways of understanding our existence and reality. We share this universe with these shadow entities, after all, so understanding more about them is to actually learn more about ourselves.

Continue to walk with me…

Introduction to the First edition

I see shadow people. And it's never been a dream.

One of my very first paranormal experiences in this life was a physical interaction with a shadow person in the middle of the night. Of course, I didn't know that's what the entity was called at the time since I was only about eight or nine years old when it happened. I thought there was an intruder in our house and he was about to kill me. That's what crosses your mind at that age, but of course, I'm still alive to tell the tale. I will never forget, however, the unusual thing it did to me when it approached me and how it had absolutely no face. Having happened at the age it did, one in which I was still rather impressionable, the event was certainly a major catalyst in pointing me down the paranormal path and helping me become the person I am today.

I first recorded that encounter with a shadow person in print in the anthology *Encounters With The Paranormal: Personal Tales Of The Supernatural* in 2014, have followed it up with informational videos on the Haunted Road Media YouTube channel (http://www.youtube.com/hauntedroadmedia), have given presentations on the subject at public speaking engagements and conferences, and the enthusiastic response has been quite interesting and eye-opening. Enclosed in these pages are many of those responses as well as the ensuing research that has prevailed since.

As you read this book, keep in mind that everything we think we know about shadow people is purely theoretical. There are a plethora of fantastic ideas out there about who or what shadow people may be, where they come from, and what they're looking to do, but until we actually sit down with a shadow person and ask those specific questions we are always going to be in the mode of speculation and conjecture. We simply don't have that exclusive interview with a shadow person to get the hard facts, and there are no remains or ancient fossils to unearth and study. What we have to work with are people's experiences, folklore, the stories and reports of shadow people interactions that, while having varying similarities, are all different to one degree or another. That said, no matter what I write in this book today, I reserve the right to change my mind.

That's not a cop out. We're still in *Exploration Mode* with shadow people. We are still observing and learning more about what these beings may be, so what we know today is different than what we knew 20 years ago and is different than what we're going to know 20 years from now. For example, Graham Hancock in his 1995 best seller *Fingerprints Of The Gods* used the idea of earth crust displacement as one of his central theories concerning lost civilizations. In 2015, that central theory in his follow-up *Magicians Of The Gods* had changed to a global cataclysm via comet impact. When asked in an interview about the discrepancy, Hancock simply pointed to the passage of two decades, how much new information can be unearthed during that time, and stated he had simply changed his mind. We don't need to pigeon-hole ourselves into one specific idea our entire lives. So, consider this a living document, one that is going to be continuously updated as we learn more about these shadow entities in the forthcoming years and decades.

What are shadow people? That's the biggest question surrounding these mysterious entities, and we still don't have very many clear answers. Are they aliens? Are they time travelers? Are they just dark-colored ghosts? Perhaps they are none of these … or perhaps they are even all!

As human beings, we like to categorize things and shadow people have been no different. I've encountered scores of books, web sites, and articles that have tackled this task, and this work will make no exception in Part I. It's a necessary evil of being human – people want to understand information in a way in which they're familiar with consuming it. We'll start off with some of the basics about shadow people, defined categories of characteristics that many in the field like to place each kind, and share with you from people of all walks a number of personal shadow experiences.

Once we've ingested this information, we can branch out into some of the more esoteric theories about who or what shadow people are, the relationship between shadow people and sleep paralysis, as well as some of the deeper questions about what they want, or if they're all evil and malicious like some believe.

I encourage you to keep an open mind, to leave the preconceptions at the door, and if you're going to be a skeptic, make sure it's a healthy dose of skepticism and not a completely polarized position. Along the way, we'll cover *many* different theories, and you can ultimately decide for yourself which ones you do or don't believe.

This is a journey, an adventure into the supernatural, down the rabbit hole, which we will explore together.

Walk with me…

PART I

Types Of Shadow People

That I now saw aright I could not and would not doubt; for the first flashing of the candles upon that canvas had seemed to dissipate the dreamy stupor which was stealing over my senses, and to startle me at once into waking life.

—Edgar Allan Poe, “The Oval Portrait”

Chapter 1

The Humanoid Figure

I was young, very young, perhaps eight or nine years old, the night I was scared speechless. I had been in bed in the midst of a dead sleep when something had suddenly awoken me. It hadn't been a sound, a roaring engine down the road or some random object falling off my dresser onto the hard wood floor of my bedroom. No, it was a presence. It was the middle of the night and the house was deathly still, dark save for the light from the street lamp slinking through the window and the soft glow of the *Peanuts* nightlight against the far wall. My eyes adjusted to the dim lighting and looked down the length of my bed. That's when I saw it.

In the corner of my bedroom, between my closet door and the window overlooking the driveway below, stood a shadowy figure. It was as tall as a man with vague features of a face, but nothing else discernable. I couldn't even tell if it was wearing clothes.

For a long while we stared at each other, I at it and it at me. Part of me hoped it would just go away, perhaps slide into the open closet doorway and just disappear. Then, perhaps, I could just chalk the incident up to a strange dream in the middle of the night. But that's not what happened.

The shadowy figure approached me where I lied and hovered over me. Its presence blocked out the light that filtered in from outside and the world around me grew dark and heavy. I still could not see any features the shadow may have borne. It was dark and ominous and as quiet as the dead. Then it reached for me.

I tried to scream, but couldn't. My mouth gaped open and all my muscles tightened as I struggled to let loose with a cry to my parents for help. My body failed me while shadowy hands took hold of me. I was frightened out of my mind not knowing what this creature had in mind to do with me. I was absolutely helpless, but its next actions made no sense.

The shadow grabbed my arms and pulled them across my body, yanking my wrists up to my neck. I continued to try to scream, but still nothing came out. What was this thing going to do with me? Why had it crossed my arms? I almost felt like I was choking.

It let go of me then and rose from my bed. It turned from me and exited my bedroom door, which was directly to my right. I rotated my head and watched as it suddenly ran down the hall to the linen closet, opened it, and then darted inside, closing the door behind it. I lied there motionlessly for a long moment, arms still crossed, mouth still gaping open trying to scream over what had just happened to me.

Finally, I was able to climb out of my bed and shuttle over to my parents' bedroom directly across the hall. I woke them from their slumber and told them what had happened, but like all good parents they were comforting and reassuring and told me it was all just a bad dream. I slept with them the rest of the night.

The humanoid figure type of shadow person is probably the most common type of shadow person reported and is the first one in which I'd had an interaction. These types of entities are simply described as appearing in the shape of a person, generally a tall man, with no discernable features. Everything about these entities is black. There are no eyes to see, no nose or mouth, nor even any clothing to view. Typically, the humanoid figure just stands and stares at you, perhaps from the corner of the room or from the end of one's bed, so having a physical interaction with one is quite out of the norm. In fact, they typically don't seem to have an actual physical form.

Many people report simply turning on a light switch or a bedside lamp and the shadow person is suddenly gone. I've had one person reach out to me about an encounter in which he'd actually shot at one of these strange entities. He thought an intruder was in his room, warned the person he saw standing in the corner that he had a gun in his nightstand drawer, and when it didn't move, he grabbed that gun and opened fire. When he turned on the light nothing stood in the corner nor was lying on the floor in a pool of its own blood, but there were clean bullet holes in the wall from the shots he fired. Did he really see someone standing in the corner? What's more, why could he shoot through the shadow person while mine was solid enough to be able to grab and manipulate my arms?

His assumptions were not far off from what my young mind had ascertained. At eight or nine years old, I had absolutely no idea what a shadow person was. When I saw that tall, dark figure standing in the corner I thought there was an intruder in the house and he was going to kill me. I'd seen enough movies at that point that I knew I had about enough time to gasp before I was quickly extinguished. But that's not what happened. So, what did this thing want?

It was first suggested to me by psychic medium Tracey Lockwood that, perhaps, this entity thought I was deceased and it was putting me into a burial pose. It's an interesting suggestion to say the least. I address this idea more in depth in Chapter 21 on whether or not shadow people are evil, but I think the question about what these entities want is one we need to keep in mind as we continue our examinations. What did this particular entity want beside stare at me and manipulate my arms? Were its motives *really* diabolical?

The Shadow of Kampsville Grade School

The Kampsville grade school in Kampsville, Illinois, is a small, one-story building nestled in the foot of a limestone bluff next to the Illinois River. A depression era building constructed in 1938, it was placed in what had been an archaeological dig site from early federal exploration efforts during the 1920s in the area for Native American artifacts and their origins. To this day, you can still see the terraces in the landscape from where the dig had been. It is no wonder the Kampsville grade school is haunted.

We have witnessed a plethora of paranormal activity at this old school, including phantom footsteps from the second floor when there is no second floor, the apparition of a woman at the bottom of the basement stairs, voices clearly talking to us, and more, but one of the greatest moments was the shadow person we caught on camera in the gymnasium.

One of the most haunted areas of the school is near the doorway that leads from the gym to the boy's locker room and stairs that lead down to the basement. From here we had heard a number of disembodied footsteps and voices, and there was routinely the sense of uneasiness in that area. During one particular investigation, it felt like somebody was toying with us. We consistently heard noises coming from the area of the doorway only for them to stop when we came near and pick back up across the gym over by the bleachers. This went back-and-forth for a little while like a game of cat-and-mouse. Eventually, we gave up and continued the investigation elsewhere in the building, but our review of the footage we captured revealed something truly significant.

In a video clip that panned the gymnasium from where we sat in the bleachers, a short shadow figure could be seen pacing near the doorway to the boy's locker room. Due to the darkness of the room at the time, we did not notice that shadow figure with our own eyes, but it is clearly visible in the video footage. Granted, the video footage is also dark since we were using no additional light source at the time, but it's plainly there. The photo included here has been lightened in order for the image to print better within this book, but the raw video footage of the moment can be viewed on the Haunted Road Media channel at: https://youtu.be/pQbiRiQxAqw

Some will argue that the image is a bit grainy — in fact, they already have — but consider the situation. It was a low-light environment using a small Canon Vixia HD camcorder with no additional light source other than what filtered in through the windows from behind the stage. Yet, the shadow person is plainly visible, especially in the actual video footage which lasts several seconds and in which you can actually see this figure walking.

So, who or what was it? We still don't know, but our belief at this point is a human spirit appearing in shadowy form and not a "real" shadow person. In height comparisons we conducted on a return trip, paranormal investigator Shana Wankel stood approximately where the shadow had lingered in the footage, and we determined that the top of the figure would have come up to about her chest, about the height of a 10 or 11-year-old child. Was this the incomplete manifestation of a child spirit? And what's the difference between this type of manifestation and a true shadow person? We'll explore this topic in Chapter 13.

Shawn's Story

Are shadow people always visible? Are they able to be active at a location without actually being visible and then later manifest into a shadowy form?

Shawn Gilmore grew up in a haunted apartment in which he experienced plenty of paranormal activity, and he moved back there for a time in his young adulthood. It was during this return after all the other paranormal activity he'd already experienced there that he witnessed a tall shadow person.

I had just moved my TV and couch into my bedroom from the storage unit, so we decided to watch a couple movies instead of fishing that night. A couple years later, my friend told me that after I had fallen asleep watching one of the movies that night, he had to use the bathroom. The bathroom in my bedroom was out of service, so my buddy went to use the bathroom in the hallway that was across from my old bedroom. When he went to open the door to the bathroom, he noticed that the light was on and the door was locked. Thinking that someone was in the bathroom, he sat on my couch where he could see when they were done and left the bathroom. He said that a half hour later no one came out and the light stayed on. A while later, he noticed that the light was turned off. He thought it was odd because no one ever came out of the bathroom, but he got up and tried to open the door, and it was unlocked. He stated that is why he never came back over to that place.

At that time, I would still enter my room and say out loud, "This is my space and you are not welcome here! Stay out!" Only then would I close my door. In this bedroom, it was different. After I would do that, I would feel very uneasy. It was like I was upsetting the spirit. So, I stopped demanding it to stay out, and I also stopped closing the bedroom door all of the way. Then one night, I was in bed trying to go to sleep. I was lying in my bed with my eyes open when I suddenly saw a tall shadow figure walk into my room. The dark shadow figure walked across my room, turned and looked at me, then took a couple more steps and disappeared into the walk-in closet.

I am not exactly sure how tall it was. It was definitely taller than the doorway, and it had long arms and was darker than the room was with all of the lights turned off. It also had no face that I could see. I was petrified. I rolled over so that I was facing the wall. I was a 23 or 24-year-old man, and I hid under my blankets like a child until the sun came out the next morning.

It's hard to know whether this shadow person had also been responsible for the bathroom incident his friend witnessed, but perhaps it's possible. Likewise, it's difficult to know whether this entity was the cause for all the paranormal activity that frequently occurred in this apartment throughout Shawn's childhood, which he explains in further detail in *Encounters With The Paranormal: Volume 4*. Let's keep it tucked away in the back of our minds as we continue our examination of shadow people.

CHAPTER 2

WEARING MANY HATS

The hat-wearing shadow is probably the most feared type of shadow person out of all the varying kinds of these types of supernatural entities. In terms of pure horror, the crawler is probably the "scariest" – we'll get to that in Chapter 7 – but since that particular phenomenon isn't reported nearly as often as "the hat man," as he's been called for several decades, the lidded one gets the nod.

The hat man is, essentially, a type of humanoid figure shadow person who also wears a hat, usually a fedora, or sometimes a top hat or a wide-brimmed piece. I've heard one account in which a hat-wearing shadow was seen wearing an archer-style hat like something out of Robin Hood. Many times, a hat man's entire appearance will seemingly take on a particular type of style. For instance, the shadow person wearing the fedora will often don a trench coat while those seen wearing a top hat may also be wearing a cape. Details of the clothing are usually sketchy since everything about the entity is still black, however it's the general outline of the being that usually gives one a sense of what these entities might be wearing. Sometimes, the clothing in its shadow form may also be seen moving as we'll learn in the following account.

These different styles, however, don't seem to correlate with any one particular goal. In other words, just because the shadow person is wearing a fedora it doesn't necessarily mean that it's there to terrorize you. Similarly, just because it's wearing a top hat it doesn't necessarily mean that it's only there to be an observer. It may have some other agenda in mind. One really doesn't know until the situation is at hand.

Tonia shared with us her encounter with a hat man, a shadow figure wearing a top hat, specifically.

Tonia's Story

My experience took place in the early 90s in a small rural town in Iowa. I had just recently divorced from my husband who had been very abusive to me and our animals as well. I had gone out earlier in the day and purchased a new alarm clock so that I didn't oversleep again and get into trouble at work. I placed the new alarm across the room on my dresser, far enough away that I would have to get up to shut it off.

The next morning when the alarm went off, I felt as if someone was watching me, and when I opened my eyes, I found a dark shadow looking at me very closely, directly into my face. I screamed, and the shadow stood and ran for the closed window with his cape swooshing from his quick departure. This shadow didn't have any facial features that I could make out, but it did appear to have a top hat and a cape for his coat.

I did find many years later that my house had been One-Eyed Jack's Mortuary in the 1900s. Was it One-Eyed Jack checking to see if I was ready to go?

While the shadow wearing a hat takes on a number of different guises, it's not the hat that instills fear in people. A hat man-type entity seems to have some sort of intense aura about him which he uses to terrorize his victims. He may just stand in the doorway and stare you down, paralyzing you in place with fear, or he may enter the room flanked by other shadow entities, usually humanoid figures. Some believe hat men feed off this negative energy like an emotional vampire.

An emotional vampire is a term generally used for toxic people who drain us of our energy like a parasite and leave us feeling emotionally exhausted. This type of person can cause one to feel depressed, anxious, frightened, or in pain, dramatically affecting the person's mental and, ultimately, physical well-being. While encountering an emotional vampire, one's entire body can react, including increased heart rate, sweaty palms, and an intense ache in one's gut and/or heart that something is drastically wrong. These are the same toxic traits typically ascribed to hat-wearing shadows.

The way the man with the hat seems to instill this fear is through some sort of thought transference. It doesn't speak. It doesn't utter a word, except perhaps, through telepathic transmission. It impresses its intended will upon its target … or prey. One such account from Cory describes this type of encounter with a hat man.

Cory's Story

I've always had a propensity for weird shit. The hat man is no different than anything else. It communicated through touch, I guess, something like telepathy. It wanted to feel being in a body. I had a feeling it wanted to be specific with its infinity.

If I'm being honest, I associated the experience more with aliens. I don't think it wanted my body. I think it wanted to explain its intrusion. Mine felt curious … cold, electric, and alien.

It started with fear. I wanted to beat the fear, but I figured it was either testing me or needing to eat something. So, once I stopped being afraid, I asked what the fuck it was doing in my room. However, I am still terrified of other beings I've seen.

I'm pretty sure the closest analogy I can give is it was hacking into the simulation and wanted to play the game it exploited. The way it was explained to me later is that we live in a simulation and they hack into it. They shouldn't. It's like a drug.

Cory's remarks about his hat man experience being like something that was hacking into a simulation is extremely interesting and will be explored more in depth in Chapter 16, "Shadows In The Matrix." For now, the take away here is that his hat man entity tried to instill fear through the use of telepathy and touch. This shadow person actually touched Cory and it's why I was so interested in contacting Cory for his story since I had also once been touched by a shadow figure.

Another account that may shed some light on how hat men instill fear is from Michelle LeBaron during an investigation at the Washoe Club in Virginia City, Nevada, a historic saloon with a reputation for being extremely haunted. Michelle aka "The Ghost Magnet," is a well-known paranormal investigator we've twice interviewed on our *Edge Of The Rabbit Hole* livestream show. It was on our January 30, 2018, broadcast in which she described her hat man experience at the Washoe Club as the paranormal experience that has affected her the most.

Michelle's Story

Abridged Transcript from "Michelle LeBaron Ghost Magnet"
Edge Of The Rabbit Hole, *January 30, 2018*

I'm one of the lucky few that have captured this man on photo. He is about six-five, six-six, very tall. I don't know why it's like that, but it's like they're always wearing a duster and a cowboy hat. He's just so powerful he keeps the other spirits at bay. There's a child there, a little boy [spirit], and a few women [spirits] that he won't let speak to you unless he allows it. He has shown himself to me, and it frightened me.

I was in the ballroom and [a fellow investigator] said, "Come with me." I asked, "Where are we going?" and she said, "I want you to come in this room and tell me what you feel."

I was looking in there and I didn't see anything, and I turned around, and she was gone. I was calling out her name, then I looked back in the room, then I turned back around, and she ... it was pitch black. It looked like she had moved forward, but what it was is that there was a huge, dark shadow man – a big mass – and it had engulfed her. She didn't even move forward, it moved back which made it look like she was coming forward. And I screamed; I was so terrified. I had never been so scared in my whole life.

We both went back into the ballroom, and I had people help calm me down. [The other investigator] didn't feel it, she didn't hear me call her name, she didn't remember any of it.

When we had calmed down, I felt I needed to walk over by the stairwell where the shadow was. I walked over there alone, and I put my hand on the end of the stairwell and I turned around and looked down the hall. I could see it on the wall; I could see him standing ... I saw him moving like this [pushes her hands back and forth] And then I heard pulsating, "Whoo, whoo, whoo."

I called it, I said, "I gotta get out of here. I can't deal with this anymore."

This frightened me. To this day ... ugh.

I think it was not human. Just from the energy I felt from it, it was not human to me.

Michelle's observation of the pulsating energy is extremely intriguing. Is this pulse energy the way the hat man instills its fear upon people, sending out waves of negativity and toxicity in order to feed on the vigor returned? Is this how the physical manifestation of an emotional vampire would actually consume its victims?

In early spring 2020, while conducting research for his book *Haunted Hotels of New England*, paranormal author Sam Baltrusis contacted me for some input about a hat man he frequently encounters in Salem, Massachusetts. It's a very intriguing manifestation since Sam believes he has significantly connected with this hat-wearing being, to the point that this entity will actually interfere with his presentations and interviews while he's telling the story of the encounter. When we invited Sam as a guest on our *Edge of the Rabbit Hole* livestream show that September, there was sudden freezing on Sam's side once he started talking about the moment he first saw the shadow person. A month later, I was interviewing Sam on a Zoom call for *The Shadow Dimension* docu-series, and once again, even after having purchased a new computer, Sam experienced technical failures during his story of a hat man encounter. I've included a transcript of part of that interview below:

Sam Baltrusis Shadow Dimension Zoom Interview

October 20, 2020

Sam: Back in 2016–2017 I was working for a hotel in Salem, Massachusetts. It was a new hotel opening up in a very historic building on Essex Street in the middle of downtown Salem. I work as a night auditor while I write my books, so I find that working as an auditor really works cohesively with my writing schedule. That year, I was working for multiple tours in Salem, including the House of Seven Gables, the Turner Ingersoll Mansion, and also giving historical tours in Salem. I thought, ok, it's after October –

[Sam's picture on the screen suddenly freezes]

Mike: Oh, kind of lost you. I lost you, Sam.

[Sam's picture unfreezes, but still no audio]

I got your video, but all the audio is gone.

[Audio returns]

Ok, now I hear you.

Sam: Ok, it's doing it again. You know, I find that every time I talk about the man in the hat that something happens.

Mike: Yeah, I remember [you] talking about that when we had you on the show, that every single time – and we were having some glitches when you were telling the story then, too.

Sam: I really do think it's connected. I bought a new computer for this and it's still acting up. I have not had any problems except for me talking about the man with the hat.

So, back when I was working for the hotel ... It was a nice boutique hotel in the middle of Salem, Massachusetts. I've written two books on Salem, so I knew a lot about the history. The first few nights when I worked by myself, I thought there was a weird energy to the building, so my first experience with what seemed to be a sort of an apparition was this black smoke that was forming in the lobby area near the elevator. I was sitting at my desk writing some stuff about the Salem Witch Trials and I looked over to the right and I saw what looked like black smoke kind of move down by the elevators.

Now, I thought maybe it was smoke coming in from outside – checked my glasses to make sure I saw what I saw – I definitely saw black smoke.

The next night, I looked over and saw the same black mass. This was around 2:00 – 3:00 in the morning during the overnight shift. What was interesting this time – it looked like it was going to the elevator, the elevator mysteriously opens, the black mask goes into the elevator and goes down to the basement like it was taking an elevator ride to the basement.

Now, I will say this – the elevator had kind of a mind of its own. It would open mysteriously even though no one was pushing the buttons, and what was even more fascinating about the elevator and then that entity going into the elevator, you have to have a special code to go into the basement.

Then I heard what sounded like banging on the elevator. [I was thinking] maybe it was somebody that got stuck in the elevator. They wanted to go to the basement to see it or maybe it's a construction worker, or something like that – at 2:00 – 3:00 o'clock in the morning – which would be very odd.

So, I go into the elevator, go down to the basement to check out what it was ... I did go through the area that was creepy which is covered in tarps and sawdust and all sorts of things. I looked down to the ground, and it looked like there were footprints on the ground as well. I went to the back of that hotel's basement area, which is where the tunnels would have been that connected the seaport area to the basement, and it was all covered in brick.

I did hear what was a moaning sound, but it wasn't a good moan, like someone was on the other side.

Then I hear what sounded like someone banging metal, like

they're taking a hammer and hitting metal really hard, and I think maybe someone is breaking in. This is too strange to be happening.

I run upstairs. I look outside to check the stores that are right next to the hotel, which is a bookstore and also there's a gift shop that's right next to the hotel as well.

That is when I see what has haunted me for years. I look into the window of the store and then I see what looks like a man in the window – and it looked like it was wearing a hat.

Now, the difference between what other shadow people that I've seen in the past and this shadow person is it had red glowing eyes. I did notice ...

[Sam's picture on the screen suddenly freezes again]

Mike: Broke up again.

[remains frozen]

Again, once you start talking about the hat man, there we go. We lost you at red glowing eyes.

[remains frozen]

Sam? Sam?

[unfreezes]

Sam: ... I connected. [stops talking and shakes head]

Mike: Yeah, we lost you again. Once you started talking about red glowing eyes ...

Sam: I think that's significant, Mike. I really do. I'll tell you, Mike, if I try to mention the man with the hat at lectures, no matter what I'm trying to do it always happens around that point. And I do think it's very significant that the man in the hat doesn't want me to tell the story.

So, when I looked right into the red glowing eyes I connected with this entity telepathically. It was basically saying, "Can you see me?"

[And I said], "Yes, I can see you."

And then it sort of darted off to the back of the store. What's interesting about that is I then heard a blood-curdling scream down the street on Essex Street, and I run down the street to see what the blood-curdling scream was, and there was nobody there.

This was a beginning of a relationship with the man with the hat. That was the first encounter that I've had with him, but I've had multiple encounters, whether I'm giving tours or staying at a hotel in Salem or just visiting Salem, I've encountered this man with a hat multiple times.

Sam's case is fascinating since the phenomena does affect him outside of Salem and even when he doesn't physically see this shadow with the hat. It's seemingly always around to one degree or another, as Sam said, having some sort of connection with him. Sam also communicated with this entity through some sort of telepathy or thought transference which we'll talk more about in Chapter 19. For now, tuck that tidbit away in the back of your mind.

Another interesting hat man story was conveyed to me by one family at a paranormal expo in which I spoke about the subject. They reported their daughters being frequented by a hat-wearing shadow who would simply stand near one of the girls' beds at night. It seemed rather attracted to the oldest, who of the three girls, was the one who experienced the most activity, and it was next to her bed in which it would usually stand, staring down at her. She saw it with her own eyes while her sister from her own bed across the room also observed it, simultaneously. For those that like to say shadow people are just hallucinations, these girls were certainly not having the exact same hallucination at the exact same time.

A few years later, the family moved from the house, and the visits from this hat man ceased. This is interesting. While this particular shadow entity was drawn to the one particular girl it appears it was not "attached" to her and didn't follow her to the new house. Without talking to the new owners, we can only speculate that this hat man shadow entity remained at the house to, perhaps, observe the next family entering the home, perhaps standing next to the bed of one of their children. Was this hat man, instead, attached to the house? Or do we look at it another way, and perhaps, it wasn't attached to the house, but rather, assigned to it?

Another interesting trait regarding hat-wearing shadows is that they sometimes appear to be the leader of other shadow people. Many experiencers have reported witnessing a hat man flanked by two other shadow entities, usually humanoid figures, as if an entire troupe has decided to enter their room to dine. Is there some sort of hierarchy within the dimension of the shadows that the hat man remains at the forefront?

Men in Black

In 1952, Albert K. Bender established the International Flying Saucer Bureau during what was known as the great UFO "Flap" that year. He published a quarterly journal for this organization called *Space Review* which reported UFO and extraterrestrial encounters witnessed across the country. Just a year after he started the IFSB, an organization that immediately spread world-wide with offices in the UK and Australia, Bender suddenly shut everything down. Many believed he was visited by what have become known as "the Men in Black," beings who threatened his organization and journal, and insisted he no longer talk about these kinds of phenomena. Bender shared vague parts of his experience with the Men in Black with Gray Barker who reported the encounter in his 1956 book *They Knew Too Much About Flying Saucers*, and the IFSB founder stepped back from his UFO research.

In 1962, however, Bender reemerged with his own book *Flying Saucers and the Three Men* in which he told the full story of his encounter with the Men in Black. Late one night Bender entered into his bedroom when suddenly three dark, shadowy hat-wearing beings with glowing eyes materialized through his wall. Using a form of thought transference, these beings communicated that they wanted Bender to stop his UFO research immediately, which he did. Accompanied with an aroma of sulphur, these entities frightened Bender so much that he was unable to eat for three days.

Bender stated these beings were extraterrestrials who were harvesting resources from the water in Antarctica over the course of 15 years and could not be discovered, which is why they demanded he shut down the IFSB and he didn't publish his own book about the encounter until 1962.

Beings from another world these three Men in Black may have been, and we will cover extraterrestrials in Chapter 17, but let's look at some of the similarities between Bender's account and those that report hat-wearing shadow phenomena.

They materialized seemingly from out of nowhere. They had a shadowy nature about themselves. They were wearing fedora-style hats. Like in Sam Baltrusis's encounter, they had glowing eyes. When in groups, shadow entities are quite often reported in threes. Like in Sam and Cory's accounts, they spoke telepathically.

I believe what Albert Bender experienced was what those who have encountered the hat-wearing shadow entities report experiencing. While these encounters could certainly be extraterrestrial in nature, they definitely have the aura of the supernatural attached and certainly seemed to be linked to each other in some fashion. I believe there are other Men in Black encounters which are a controlling, shadowy part of our government flexing its muscle, real human beings with some secret agenda. Having spent a brief amount of time at NSA (the National Security Agency), I've seen some of it. But what Albert K. Bender, and Sam Baltrusis, and Cory, and Michelle, and Tonia, and so many others have experienced for centuries is something not of this plane of existence or world.

Whether hat men are simply humanoid spirits wearing some sort of clothing to guise themselves like humans or are another type of shadow entity entirely is still truly unknown. Any viewpoint stating definitively one way or the other is really just one person's conjecture, although that person may be correct to one degree or another. The hat man, along with his (or her – who says it can't be female?) intentions, remains one of the most mysterious of all the shadow entities.

Chapter 3

Eyes Of A Stranger

Most commonly, shadow people are seen without eyes. Usually, they are completely devoid of features — no eyes, no nose, no mouth. Nothing. Everything is black. However, on occasion, some shadow people do present eyes which are quite striking to witness since the color is heavily contrasted against the sheer blackness of the rest of the entity. Why do some shadow people have eyes, and what do the colors mean?

The most notorious of the colored-eyed shadow people are the ones with red eyes. These are generally considered more nefarious in nature, devious entities who strike fear into the victims they oppress, much like the hat man. Some people will go so far as to call these red-eyed shadow people evil.

Monster In The Closet

Personally, I have not seen the shadow person with red eyes, but one of the biggest cases I've worked on to date involved a dark, malevolent entity with red eyes in the closet of a young adult woman in Edmond, Oklahoma, and was featured on the television show *The Haunted*, which originally aired on Animal Planet and has now been broadcast in syndication on multiple networks, including Netflix for a time, and even one network in France. Titled "Monster In The Closet," this episode focused on the haunting of Talasyn, a young woman who was being terrorized by a figure she routinely saw standing in her closet doorway which sported red eyes and a nasty disposition that included impressing self-destructive thoughts upon her.

According to Talasyn, "As the days went on after I saw the red-eyed thing I was in a very, very, very depressed state. All I felt was … I want to die. I want to hurt myself. I want to kill myself. I'm not worth the space I take up on Earth – thoughts that I never had in my entire life."

This entity had first been seen years beforehand by her brother, Travis, who stated, "I wake up at three o'clock in the morning, and I'm just frozen solid. I can see my breath. And I'm going, it's not cold enough to see my breath. All of a sudden, I hear a voice, and it goes, 'Not my fault!' I looked straight into my closet, and I couldn't believe what I was staring at. There was a dark, dark entity with red eyes. I was petrified. I just started yelling, 'Get out! You're not welcome here!' Almost instantly, the room got really calm. I had never experienced anything like that in my life. … I didn't tell anyone for a while. I just didn't know what to say. Shortly thereafter, I moved out. It was very nice to get out of that house."

Without knowing what her brother had experienced, including a wildly chaotic paranormal event he described as a wrestling match between two people in his room he couldn't see, Talasyn eventually moved into Travis's old bedroom. It wasn't long before she also began experiencing the activity.

"When I had gone to bed," she recounted, "Jasmine [the cat]

was asleep in the bed with me, and I remember hearing something like feet shuffling. Jasmine jerked from a dead sleep and was sitting straight up, ears pointed up, and growling on the bed. And I just heard something whisper, 'Tal.' That's my nickname that everybody calls me. And then I saw a really, really dark shadow up in the corner above my closet, and right in the middle of it were two red eyes. It just sat there and looked straight at me. I was scared to death."

With new prey in the bedroom, this red-eyed entity attacked Talasyn's psyche, instilling thoughts in her mind of self-infliction which she'd never had before. "The thoughts I was getting in my head weren't mine because I would never kill myself, I would never want to hurt myself. I couldn't figure out why I was feeling that way when I've never felt that way before. It was always the same thoughts and feelings. It was just like you're being invaded."

Although she didn't leave home like her brother had done, she unknowingly followed his lead in not saying a word. "The only time I felt happy is [sic] if I was away from the house. I didn't say anything to anybody about what was going on with me."

Talasyn's behavior began changing, and her mother, Susan, would hear her cry out from her room sometimes.

According to Susan, "There were times that Talasyn wouldn't be herself. She would get very hostile. She didn't sound like herself, she didn't look like herself. Her behavior had changed that [sic] I was afraid. Something was wrong."

Finally, after an incident one night in which Susan was held down in bed by something unseen, her husband, Danny, shocked to wake to her thrashing, called a family meeting. This meeting was a revelation to the family, all shocked to discover they'd all been experiencing paranormal activity at the house for twenty years, and the stories started flowing forth. The most pressing matter at hand, of course, was Talasyn's torment from the dark entity with red eyes as she continued to drown deeper and deeper in her despair.

The paranormal investigative team I was with at the time was called in to help determine what was going on at the house and to help put a stop to the negative activity that was transpiring within. Our research uncovered a number of tragedies at the house: two suicides, one intentional and one accidental, and an attempted suicide during a violent domestic dispute that had gone terribly wrong. Part of our investigation was in determining whether the entity tormenting Talasyn was one of those who had died on the property – in Talasyn's bedroom, no less – or something else, something that may have been at the heart of, not just Talasyn's despair, but also of those previously in the home who had also suffered. Were they driven to do what they did by an outside force? Through meticulous questioning, experimentation, and research, we determined that the dark entity terrorizing Talasyn was not a previous resident of the house. It was something else, something older than the house itself.

We never did actually see the entity with red eyes during our half dozen investigations of the home, but there was a shadow entity of a different ilk I witnessed in Talasyn's room which I'll cover in Chapter 5. It's possible that this other shadow was an incomplete manifestation of the entity with red eyes, but we'll never know for sure.

Renowned paranormal investigator and demonologist Carl Johnson was brought into the case to determine specifically what this entity was and, ultimately, to drive it from the home. While Carl was on a phone call with Susan, Talasyn walked into the room and demanded to know who was on the phone. Once she was told Carl was on the other end, something came forth from Talasyn calling Carl "The Chastiser" and insisting Susan hang up the phone and not let him come to the house. Talasyn was then propelled forward into the kitchen, face reddening, and she crashed to the floor, choking. Once Susan hung up the phone, her daughter calmed down. Talasyn remembered none of this happening.

Drawing upon his decades of experience, his interactions with the family, and our detailed reports, Carl deemed this dark, malevolent entity with red eyes a wraith.

During an interview on our *Edge of the Rabbit Hole* livestream show on the Haunted Road Media YouTube channel, he explained, "I had said it was wraith-like, and I thought that described it the best of anything, a wraith. Something that's quasi-human in appearance in that aspect, flits around very rapidly, and was black and shadowy, and that's what Talasyn was seeing in the closet."

He then further defined what a wraith is. "We say wraith – now that's kind of an archaic term, but it does indicate a form of shadow ghost, a shadow person. If it's malevolent we tend to call it a wraith. They are combative, but they tend to have an agenda. They are insidious. They have a sinister intelligence and go after somebody and target a person. It's something that knows the family, knows its victim, almost seems to have studied them. It seems bent on disrupting and destroying the family unit."

There are many things that happened the night we cleansed the home of the entity which are beyond the scope of this book, more than what the television episode showed, including doors blowing open on their own and a captured Electronic Voice Phenomenon (EVP) that said, "Die," during an intense moment when Carl was blessing Talasyn and she doubled over in pain as if she'd been punched in the gut. I'll detail this case in another work, but ultimately, the red-eyed entity was driven out and didn't return. Most importantly, Talasyn was all right and the family lived on in peace.

Perhaps it's the color red, an emotionally intense color that is associated with danger, power, passion, and evil, which causes one's blood to boil when viewing an entity with such eyes. Red is the color of strength and perseverance, it is the color of sexuality, and it is the color of ambition and determination. It is also the color of rage. However, just because a shadow person has red eyes, a color that expresses all of these fierce emotions, it doesn't necessarily mean it is going to prey upon the humans with which it comes into contact.

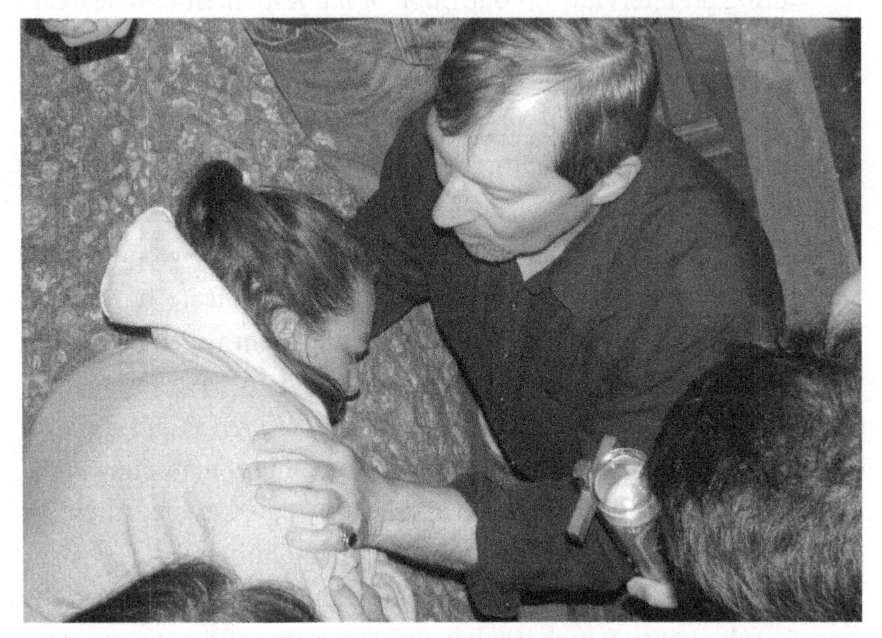

Carl Johnson helping Talasyn after she doubled over in pain.

While Talasyn had a very negative experience with a dark, red-eyed entity, others have reported shadow people with red eyes that are seemingly more ambivalent in nature. Again, we can only guess at the true intentions of most of these entities, but sometimes a red-eyed shadow person will act just like their humanoid figure counterparts and play the part of a curiosity-seeker.

In a correspondence I received from a woman named Laurie, she related to me her own personal experience with a red-eyed entity that was not malevolent. While certainly creepy, the benign nature of this incident gives pause to question just exactly what these things are trying to do.

Laurie's Story

I recently watched your YouTube video on this particular subject, and felt a strange need to make contact. I haven't come across many people, (online, or off), that have seen a shadow figure with red eyes. I am one that has.

It happened when I was 37. It was about ten in the evening, and my husband at the time and our children were already tucked away in their slumbers. We have a wall between our kitchen and living room area. Our large bay window was on the living room side. As one would assume, you'd think, okay, she was probably lying down on the couch asleep or about to fall asleep. You couldn't be more wrong. Part of me wishes that I could explain this away so easily. The other part has been intrigue since that moment occurred.

I was at the desktop computer. My bottom started feeling numb, so I stood up to stretch. I use black out curtains, by the way. Earlier that evening, once everyone was asleep, I shut all the curtains between the two main rooms except the bay window. My purpose for that was because the street light had gone out. To give you a better idea: the bay window faces the house next door, not much of a view with such a large frame. You could, however, see part of the road to the left, which is where the street light went out. The town I lived in was very small, a literal one stop sign town, not one traffic light for miles. The house that faces our bay window was empty. We had actually lived in the neighboring house first. We needed more space, and the current house was right next door and bigger. So, the neighboring house that we previously lived in was, at the time, vacant. In the current house, there is a basement with walls raised above ground about a foot or so. So, the bay window measurements, from the top of the window to the ground must have been about ten feet or so.

When the street light went out, it was very dark out there. I don't like people looking in on me, so I usually have all the curtains shut. But because the street light was out, I waited to shut that particular window so I could attempt to keep an eye out for any potential hazards. In such a small community, one street light out can be hazardous for outsiders scurrying through with bad intentions.

So, as I stood to stretch, I moved a few steps to get between the walkway between the kitchen and living room. My TV was on and sits in between the bay window and kitchen windows, so therefore, I could see my peripheral of both rooms, simultaneously. As I began to really stretch out good, I, for some reason, faced the bay window first. Now, remember when I stated that the walls of the basement are raised above ground here. When I looked out of the bay window, my arms above my head from stretching, I saw this even darker than the dark mass outside. Its mass blocked out the house next door in an area. And the eyes ... the eyes were this glowing red ... not extremely bright, but this deep red tone, partially illuminated. They were wide and didn't blink.

I found my eyes fixated on its eyes, almost taunting it to blink first, but definitely not on purpose. I felt frozen at first, almost paralyzed standing up. Just a brief moment of shock was all as I realized that these eyes weren't blinking, weren't moving, weren't changing color tones, just nothing but this blank stare.

I'm five foot, and with the ground raised up outside, it stood taller than me, with the help of the raised basement.

It was the longest ten second scare I've ever had prior to that moment, but it didn't stop there. My arms were still stretched out above my head. My thought process went from, "Oh shit, it's not disappearing." So, I quickly told myself to slowly turn as if I was just stretching and didn't see it, even though I knew it knew that I did. I turned slowly, still stretching towards my kitchen. I held that pose for about five seconds, then slowly turned back around in the hopes that it was gone. It was still there.

Now, I began to wonder what the hell I was dealing with. Again, now in complete panic mode, and not making the best decisions probably, I pushed on, slowly turning towards the kitchen. Inside my head, I kept saying, “Please don’t be there, please don’t be there,” as I began to turn back to it once again. I was astonished to see it still there for the third time. I almost bolted out of the room, but at the same time, I almost opened the door to get a better look at it or to find out what it wanted. Luckily, I did not attempt the latter. I did neither. I believe that was due to my body. It just froze.

We played the game three times. The fourth time when I turned to the kitchen I didn't turn back around so quickly. I waited what seemed like forever, but was only about a minute. Before I could turn back around to check this time, as I faced the kitchen, yes black out curtains in there as well, I swear I could feel its energy wrapping around the side of the house where the long kitchen windows were. Curtains closed, I could not see out at all, but I'm positive that those curtains didn't stop him. I could feel the presence by the kitchen windows, and then ... nothing. Just gone.

I looked this thing in the eyes, more than once on the same occasion. You may ask me if I felt that it was malevolent or benevolent. I didn't get the sense that it was there to do harm, but it was curious. I can't say if it was curious about me as a human or curious to see how I reacted to its presence in front me, sort of full throttle. To this day, and I'm now 45, I still have more questions than answers about any of it.

This story suggests that not all red-eyed entities are present to inflict harm. Although certainly creepy, this particular red-eyed shadow person seems to have done what its humanoid figure counterpart usually does – stand and stare. Was it sizing up Laurie to make a meal out of her then decided to feast on other prey, or was it simply observing and taking notes about what she was doing? Was it, perhaps, trying to deduce what a human was doing at a desktop computer? Does it even know what a computer is? Shadow person encounters always seem to leave more questions than answers.

Eyes of Another Color

It may come as a surprise to some that not all shadow people with visible eyes have red eyes. Red is certainly the color most often reported, but I've also heard stories of dark entities with yellow and even purple eyes. These acted in much the same way as their red-eyed brethren, so it's unclear as to whether the color of eyes actually has any significance to the function of the shadow person. However, just for the sake of it, we'll go ahead and quickly examine what these particular colors could mean.

Yellow: Yellow is actually the brightest color the human eye can see and is usually related to learning, stimulating our perception. For this reason and also because it's a cheerful and energetic color, it is often used for children's toys. Ironically, it is also the eye color used most often in horror movies to depict demonic possession.

Purple: Purple has long been known as the color of royalty. Since the dye was such a difficult color to produce in ancient times, it was usually only the wealthy who could afford to wear it. Purple also signifies imagination and spirituality, encouraging us to get in touch with a higher level of consciousness.

Blue: Blue is generally considered a calming color which is why it's a color typically used by hospitals and airlines. It is a quiet color, promoting physical and mental relaxation, and also symbolizes loyalty, strength, and trust. Blue eyes are rarely reported with shadow people sightings, but they have been seen.

Black-Eyed Children

I often get asked if Black-Eyed Children (BEKs for Black-Eyed Kids) are a type of shadow people, but I don't believe they are. While they are certainly extremely creepy, BEKs simply don't share many of the similar characteristics that the various kinds of shadow people have with each other.

Black-Eyed Children are strange entities often described as very pale with completely black eyes and wearing drab, almost oversized clothing. While their appearance is generally disheveled and shabby, it's the way they talk that causes alarm to most people – they're disconcertedly monotone. Appearing on your front doorstep or even at your car, they almost demand entry, but in the most peculiar way. For some unknown reason, they must be invited in, and they will say just that, "You want to invite us in," along with other methods of persuasion regarding food or will even ask to come in and watch the TV, all the while keeping monotone. The target of this encounter will feel compelled to let these children into their home or car while simultaneously feeling a great sense of alarm. Witnesses have reported that once they've refused and avert their eyes from these children they will suddenly vanish.

These sightings are quite different than shadow people encounters. First of all, BEKs are fully manifested. Their entire form is visible including facial features, hair, arms and legs, and clothing. There are no dark faces devoid of any features about BEKs; they look just like children. They're just a bit … off. Secondly, Black-Eyed Children are extremely interactive. They walk right up to a person's front door, knock on it, and *talk* to the person who answers. They will carry on an entire conversation with a person to try to persuade the target to let them in until they're denied. Shadow people don't have these stand-at-your-front-door types of conversations with people. Finally, shadow people don't need to be invited into your home. Shadow entities of all kinds will manifest in your bedroom, in your living room, in your basement – pretty much anywhere they like. They may manifest outside a window and stare in at you like Laurie described above, but they won't knock on the front door. They'll simply enter on their own accord.

Yes, Black-Eyed Children are extremely creepy, they seem to come from nowhere and disappear without a trace, and they don the disconcerting black eyes. Certainly, they are something either supernatural or interdimensional. However, they are not shadow people.

Chapter 4

The Hooded Figure

The hooded figure is another type of shadow person that is usually considered menacing in nature, though not as menacing as the hat man, yet there are a surprising number of reports in which the hooded figure has acted more benevolent in nature. Perhaps the reason so many people believe this shadow person to be evil and nefarious is because they relate the hood with the Grim Reaper.

The Grim Reaper, if it truly exists, is not a shadow person, but a different entity entirely that is a representation of death and is not really evil at all. When the Grim Reaper comes calling, it is just doing its job to collect souls when one's time on Earth has expired, serving as a *psychopomp*, a guide who helps souls find their way to the next realm. The Reaper is shrouded in black robes with a hood and it carries a scythe, and it's this appearance, one of ominous darkness and foreboding, that causes people to ask if the Grim Reaper is a type of shadow person. It is not.

Hooded shadow figures are very enigmatic and are certainly shrouded (pun intended) in mystique. What lies underneath the hood is unknown, and why they've elected to wear a hood in the first place is pure speculation and conjecture by anyone trying to determine the reason. These figures seem more physically active than other shadow entities, moving about quite freely while other shadows seem resigned to lurking in corners and staring at people.

Tammy and Tonya Hayn are twin sisters who live in rural Calhoun County in Illinois. Over the years, they've each had their share of paranormal experiences, including multiple encounters with hooded figures. They've seen first-hand that not all hooded shadow entities are created equal.

Tammy's Story

I grew up in a small town where everyone truly knew everyone. We were neighbors, family and friends. It was a pretty nice way to grow up. So, when a friend whom I had gone to school with my whole life, Shana, asked my sister, Tonya, and I if we were interested in going on a local ghost hunt/adventure how could I turn her down?

The place she suggested had a long history and the property had also been occupied by some business or another for a very long time. It had been the local grocery store while we were growing up, however, it had changed hands and eventually closed altogether. This had obviously been a place we had been to many times; it was never really scary, but in a couple areas in the back of the store it felt a little uneasy. Shana had told us some of the experiences that had happened to her and others that had toured the property. There were stories that were on the darker side, and included entities that tried to scare you away from touring it. I found this interesting but not really off-putting to me since I like to experience and judge things for myself. I try to keep a positive outlook on things instead of looking for or thinking the worst right away.

We set up an evening for our adventure. I was pretty excited about going on this ghost hunt since it would be the first one I had ever been involved with. The night before our hunt was a normal evening. I went to bed ready for a good night's sleep. Sometime in the night, I was awakened. I'm not even sure why I woke up, but as I looked toward the foot end of my bed, I saw a dark figure standing there. It was very black and seemed to have an outline as if it were wearing a hood and cloak. The dark figure had a hold of my ankles and was starting to lift me off of the bed!

Now, I started to get scared and kick my feet. As I did this, I looked toward my young son, Jacob, and husband, Darren, in the bed beside me, and all I could think was, "I hope Jacob doesn't wake up because he will be really scared!" I then looked back at this dark figure and was still kicking my feet as he (I just felt it was a male) had a hold of my ankles and was raising them off of the bed. As I began to get more panicked and frightened, I could feel the figure getting joy from my fear. In fact, the more scared I got the stronger the entity became, and I could hear it laughing. When I say it was laughing, I don't know if I could physically hear it or if I could just hear it in my mind.

I was raised Catholic and still practice my religion today. As I was panicking, I thought of something my Aunt had told me when I was younger. She once told me that, as Catholics, we believe if you are in the presence of evil or need help in any way you can call out the name of Jesus three times and he will be there for you. So, this is what I did. When I said the name of Jesus three times in a row the dark figure instantly disappeared! I believe this dark figure was trying to keep me from going on the ghost hunt the next day.

The next day, I told my sister of my experience the night before and we agreed we needed a little help from our Catholic faith. We both had a Catholic Rosary that had been blessed by Pope John Paul II, and we agreed to put it in our pockets for the investigation. As we were driving to the property, we passed a Catholic church and decided to stop in for a prayer card with the prayer to Saint Michael the Archangel printed on it, and we also put that in our pockets.

As we pulled up to meet Shana, we recited the prayer before we got out of the car. This at least made us feel protected. We met Shana, went inside, and waited for something to happen. Not a lot happened, and because Shana knew we were excited and wanted to experience something, she kind of felt responsible for nothing happening and kept saying, "This is normally a very active place, I don't know why it's so quiet tonight."

Tonya and I felt pretty guilty about this because we had our Rosaries and had said the prayer to Saint Michael for protection. We definitely felt these things were working to protect us from the dark shadow I had seen the night before. We didn't tell Shana any of this, though; we wanted to see how this investigation turned out. So, we had a fun evening, but not much activity was observed. We ran into Shana about a week later and finally came clean to her as to what I had experienced the night before our hunt and about our Rosaries and prayers. I have not been visited again by this dark shadow figure as I feel it was directly linked to the store property, and I have not had the chance to go back and visit again. As a person of Catholic faith, I definitely believe in the power of blessings and prayer.

This encounter Tammy has is, essentially, everyone's worst fear with shadow people: it got physical. It's hard to know whether or not the hooded figure she encountered had anything to do with the building they were going to investigate, but it's probable the energy she and her sister surrounded themselves with the following day kept most entities at bay during their investigation.

This second story provides a perspective from each sister about an encounter in an entirely different light.

Tammy's Story

This story begins with the birth of my baby, Jacob. Life with a newborn was pretty normal until his two-week checkup. His doctor felt something wasn't right and did some extra tests. We did bloodwork and were immediately rushed to Children's Hospital. After a very long night full of doctors, tests, and a blood transfusion, we were sent home. We found out later that if we had been even one day late for Jake's two-week appointment it would have been too late since his hemoglobin count was so low that he wouldn't have made it one more day without the transfusion.

There was no diagnosis given at that time; the doctors were just not sure what was going on. We lived with no diagnosis for a while, and then we finally had a name for his condition: Diamond Blackfan Anemia. We lived with countless blood transfusions and hospital stays, knowing a bone marrow transplant was imminent. This happened over a period of months.

As time went on, I began to see and feel a presence in my house. My husband worked nights, and I was home alone. When I would wake in the middle of the night to feed Jake, I would take him to the kitchen with me to warm his bottle. As I did this, I often would see a dark hooded shadow leave our bedroom and go down the hall to my son's room. It was solid, dark black, very tall, it reached from the floor to the ceiling and seemed to float as it moved. I had the feeling it was male but never a human. It never really frightened me; however, I had a thought occur as though someone was speaking to me: "Someone is coming to help him or help him over."

As time went on, I saw this dark figure every night and sometimes during the day. It was always out of the corner of my eye, but it never frightened me. Each time I had the same instant thought: "Someone is coming to help him or help him over."

We had an appointment coming up to meet with the bone marrow transplant team, so that when the time came, we knew what to expect. As this appointment got closer, I saw this figure more often, sometimes a couple times a day. Unbeknownst to me, my twin sister was also having experiences at her house over the same months as I.

Tonya's Story

At the time of my nephew's birth, my baby, Ryan, was two years old. Tammy had always been helping me with Ryan; she was pretty much a second mother to him. So, when Tammy had Jacob, I tried to always be there for her, because I know how much it means to have someone else love your baby like their own. I definitely always treated Jacob like my own baby in every way, so when Jake started having health problems, I was constantly worried and offered up many prayers to help us all through whatever was about to happen.

During this time, I was home alone with Ryan a lot. Every once in a while, I would catch a shadow out of the corner of my eye. Now, when I say shadow, it was not the shadow of a person. It was very tall, so tall it went from the floor to the ceiling. It was also very skinny, and somehow, I knew it was never a person. Somehow, I knew it was here because of Jake.

It always seemed to appear when I was thinking of Jake. If you've ever had to worry about someone, you know that any time you have a free moment your thoughts turn to that person. When I would see this shadow, I was never scared. I just wondered to myself if this shadow was here to help him or to take him to the other side. You would think that being home alone with a two-year-old and seeing something unexplainable would frighten me, but it never did, not one time. I would see this shadow during the night, during the day, at any time, but it was always out of the corner of my eye.

One day, Jake was at the hospital again, so my thoughts were with him throughout the day. Ryan and I were watching cartoons during the afternoon when I saw the shadow straight on. I looked up to see it peeking around a corner at us. This was the first and only time I ever saw it straight on, every other time I saw it out of the corner of my eye. To me there was no denying it – it was here for Jake.

Tammy and Tonya's Story (Told by Tammy)

This is where our stories join. We don't know if it's being sisters or being twins, but we have always told each other everything, so we both find it very strange that during these eleven months we both forgot to tell each other about seeing this shadow. Then one day we were talking, and I mentioned to Tonya, "You know, I keep seeing this shadow."

Tonya said to me, "So have I. It's tall isn't it?"

"Yes, it's as tall as the ceiling."

"It's black and real skinny."

I said, "Yes, exactly."

We had no idea until that moment that we had been seeing the very same shadow in each of our houses all those months.

As the appointment with the doctors to meet the bone marrow transplant team grew closer, each of us seemed to be seeing the shadow more frequently, which made us nervous. Was it here to help Jake get better or to help take him to the other side?

The day of the appointment was a typical visit. Jake had all the same blood work and tests done that day as he'd had done on all the other visits. The doctor had also been asking the same questions each time, but as this appointment was coming to a close, he suddenly stopped mid-sentence. He paused at an unusual point in the conversation, then turned his head as if he were listening to someone who was speaking in his ear.

The doctor said, “Let’s do one more test,” then left the room.

I looked at my husband, Darren, and said, “Well, that was strange.”

Darren agreed.

We waited for the new test results, and when the doctor entered the room he said, “We think we were wrong. We think it’s something else and not Diamond Blackfan Anemia. We think it’s Hereditary Spherocytosis.”

We sat in disbelief as he explained the new diagnosis, that while Hereditary Spherocytosis may still require blood transfusions and other issues could arise, it was definitely better than Diamond Blackfan Anemia since Diamond Blackfan Anemia will eventually turn into cancer. We could argue that the first diagnosis was actually wrong the whole time, but we feel everything changed that day.

After this appointment, neither Tonya nor I have ever seen this shadow figure again. Even though it was a dark, black shadow which most people would believe was a negative presence, we both feel it was a positive entity who was truly there to help Jake through this life event.

Later in this book, we discuss the question about whether or not shadow people are evil and how the answer to this question really is not as clear cut as most people think. These experiences by the twins clearly show two different agendas by two different hooded figures, muddying the waters for anyone trying to take a polarizing stance. These experiences leave a lot left open as to what the ultimate aim of shadow people might be. Are they here to help us or harm us?

To make matters even more confusing (or interesting, depending on your perspective), some hooded figures may not exactly be what you think they are and may have a very good reason for appearing the way they do. In her book, *My Life Amidst The Paranormal*, Cathy E. Gasch reported the helping hand of a hooded figure at the ruins of a Sixteenth Century friary called Slane Hill in Ireland. This is part of her story reprinted here, and I encourage you to seek out the full account and the rest of her paranormal experiences in her book.

Cat's Story

Reprinted from My Life Amidst The Paranormal
Published in 2015 by Haunted Road Media

I thought it was dangerous footing going up – now it was worse going down with nothing to hold on to! I had gone no more than a third of the way, when I realized that I was coming to the worst section of the tower with the stairs covered in slippery moss, so I braced myself and decided to go down one step at a time – on my butt!

Yep, sit on the step, put your feet down, sit on the step, put your feet down … one step at a time.

It was tedious but safer, or at least I thought so! Every so many steps my rear end would slip and I came down on the lower step with a thud. Ouch!

I was almost to the bottom and I could see daylight with no more than fifteen steps to go. Feeling relieved to be at the end, I stood up and decided to walk down upright – big mistake!

I had no sooner stood up when the heel of my right shoe slipped, my left leg buckled under me, and I felt my back hit the step, hard! I could see the wall getting closer to my face, my balance completely gone!

Just as I thought I was going to go down the remaining stairs on my back, "someone" grabbed my right elbow and left shoulder blade and I stopped slipping! The touch was firm but gentle and didn't let go until I managed to secure myself.

Being so stunned that I was no longer falling, I looked behind me to see who it was that had caught me, but to my shock there was no one there!

I managed to get myself seated and checked for injuries. My hands were red from being scraped, my leg ached from being twisted, and I could hear my heart beating through my ears! Catching my breath, I started shaking when I realized that I could have been seriously injured with a long way to go for help!

Somehow, I managed to stand up but then decided it would be safer for me to go down the last few steps, again on my butt. Just as I sat down, I heard the muffled sound of soft soled shoes going up the steps behind me, and I looked around to see – no one! Knowing that there was no way for anyone to be in the tower and get ahead of me in order to be behind me, I realized that the only explanation for what happened was that I had been caught by a ghost. I looked back up the stairs, still hearing the footsteps and smiled.

I finally reached the last step and walked, or rather limped, my way out of the tower and met up with my sister. After we got to the car, I told her that I had slipped and that I didn't think I should drive.

At first, she was angry with me for climbing the tower and getting injured, but when I explained that "someone" had grabbed me and prevented me from going ass over tin cups, she turned pale!

She told me that after I yelled to her from top of the tower, she had seen someone walking in the bell area below me. I told her that no one could have been walking on that level, there is no floor to walk on, but she insisted that she had seen someone wearing a "hoodie" and it bothered her that I wasn't alone up there. I tried to reassure her that no one was else was in that tower with me – at least no one alive anyway! She just shook her head at me and said nothing else.

Even though my leg was hurting, I told her I would be right back and limped my way back to the tower. I stood at the bottom of the steps and called out, “Thank you! You may have saved my life.”

When I turned to walk away, I could have sworn that I heard someone say something but I couldn’t understand what it was they had said. Was it old Gaelic? Was it Latin? Who knows? All I know is that they acknowledged my gratitude.

My sister reluctantly got behind the wheel and turned onto the main road. And though I was in pain and still shaken by the fall, I smiled at this wonderful experience!

You see, even though the friary has been abandoned since the early 1700s, I truly believe that some kindly friar or monk still roams the grounds, taking their duties to heart and lending a helping hand to those in need!

Again, we see in this story another shadow entity being helpful rather than harmful. This particular hooded figure is probably exactly what Cat thought it was – the ghost of a friar or monk. That it manifested enough to appear hooded to her sister’s eyes is rather significant, and we’ll talk more about the similarities and differences between shadow people and ghosts in Chapter 13. For now, just tuck away her story until we get there, and keep in mind that context needs to be considered when we observe these different entities.

What if your hooded figure entity is so monk-like that you also hear chanting along with its appearance? What if that appearance is also made by three of them? Such was the case for author and cartoonist Lacye Lembke when she suddenly awoke to three hooded figures standing over her bed.

According to Lacye, she was in a partial state of sleep paralysis; however, she was still able to move her head from side to side, so the paralysis wasn't complete. Her recollection of the incident is rather vivid, describing the hooded figures as wearing brown robes with large sleeves, but their hands were black as were their faces – completely black and devoid of any features. The hooded figure in the middle held out his arms as if he was reading a book, but his robes were so large that she was unable to tell what he may have actually been holding, if anything at all. They continued to chant over her body in a style that she thought was Gregorian, a type of chanting developed and used in western and central Europe during the Ninth and Tenth Centuries by the Roman Catholic Church. She said that the experience felt like it lasted 30 minutes, but it could have just as well have lasted only a few. Then, without any warning, the three figures suddenly disappeared.

Lacye's account is extremely surreal and almost sounds like something straight out of an exorcist horror movie. Were these hooded figures the spirits of real monks, conducting a ceremony as they had once done long ago, or were they some sort of interdimensional beings chanting and performing a ritual for some yet unknown reason? We can only speculate and theorize, a recurring theme when it comes to these mysterious shadow people.

Chapter 5

The Mist

The black mist, the cloud, the black smoke, they're all different terms for a very similar phenomenon – the vaporous manifestation of a shadow entity. It could roll into the room out of a hallway, self-manifest in a corner, or even rise up out of the floor. There's no one specific form for this type of shadow as this shadow has no *real* form at all, materializing into most any shape it likes then dematerializing into nothing.

My most prolific experience with "The Mist" was certainly during one of the investigations we conducted at the house in Edmond, Oklahoma, which was later featured in the "Monster in the Closet" episode of *The Haunted*, originally broadcast on Animal Planet in 2011. *The Haunted*, since it was developed for Animal Planet, targeted its storytelling model around the animals at the haunted location and how they reacted to paranormal activity. Most episodes of this show's run were, indeed, very animal-centric, but our particular episode focused more on the humans that lived at the house when it aired. Still, it became one of the most compelling and widely-received episodes of the entire run, so the production company certainly did a fine job with it. It was, as demonologist Carl Johnson who joined us for the final cleansing said, a story that could have used a two-hour episode. Thus, much to my chagrin, an important segment concerning one of the cats and a shadow entity was scrapped and only exists now as a deleted scene that was included on the DVD the production company gave the family. Fortunately, I have a copy, and I often show the clip when I give presentations and lecture about shadow people.

We investigated the Edmond house about five or six times before we filmed the cleansing night with Carl, and during one of those investigations Jasmine, the cat, started acting very skittish. She darted about the living room and dinette area, ventured into the kitchen at one point, eyes flicking to-and-fro, and eventually, she scampered to the bedroom doorway of the adult daughter, Talasyn, who was reporting most of the trouble with the entity with red eyes we spoke of in Chapter 3. There, Jasmine stopped dead in her tracks.

I had been tracking the cat and pulled up behind her in the doorway when I saw precisely why she stopped. There, in the middle of the bedroom was a large, black mass, almost cloud-like in nature. As I said in the deleted scene, "It was a massive black shadow. I was startled just because of the size of it."

Jasmine would have none of it. She immediately backed off from the room, slithered around the corner under a chair, and from what I was told, ended up somewhere on the other side of the piano in the living room. Meanwhile, I stared at this thing hovering in the middle of the room.

When I say cloud-like, I mean just that. It was just like any other misty vapor cloud you may see, almost like a small patch of fog hovering in your back yard, except that it was black. As I continued to stare and ready my camera, it began to slowly dissipate away. I did manage to snap off of a photograph, but I had the flash activated and it totally obliterated the shadow with its piercing light. When the bright light had subsided, the last remnants of the black mist were dissolving away, and my photograph was simply that of the girl's bedroom. It was a hard lesson to learn in photography during paranormal investigations, thus, I no longer use a flash.

I didn't believe this was a manifestation of the entity with red eyes Talasyn had been seeing in her closet. This seemed to be something else, some other sort of energy trying to take form in her room. It's hard to say whether it was really even definitively negative in nature, although it certainly seemed ominous and heavy. The cat got out of there as quickly as it could, after all. Perhaps, standing in the doorway holding a camera was just the dumb human being a dumb human and not realizing what sort of nefarious entity could possibly be looming ahead. Nothing malicious happened, however, and whatever it had been was gone within moments after it had first been seen.

Speaking of Carl Johnson, when he and his brother, Keith, first investigated the Perron house, the haunted farmhouse from which the movie *The Conjuring* is based, he seems to have seen something similar. Carl and Keith are the ones to have originally alerted Ed and Lorraine Warren about the infamous case. Carolyn Perron answered an ad their paranormal investigative team, PIRO (Parapsychology Investigative Research Organization), had placed in the newspaper, but there is some controversy here since Carolyn states she never answered an ad in the paper, and PIRO surprised the family when they showed up at the house. Did the house or something else in the universe reach out to the Johnson's and beckon them to come?

In any case, this is quite different than what the film depicts, and for a full account of the events that transpired during the ten years the Perron's lived in the house, I highly recommend the *House Of Darkness House Of Light* book trilogy by the family's eldest daughter, Andrea Perron.

Prior to the Warren's investigation, Carl and Keith visited several times to get a sense of the activity and to see what they could do to help. While many things happened during their investigations, one of the things Carl witnessed was a black shadow without form on the second floor.

On July 28, 2019, I conducted a phone interview with Carl to talk about his experiences with shadow people, including the "smoke" he witnessed at the farmhouse. This was prior to the filming he and Keith conducted with *Ghost Adventures*, the episode which aired on Halloween 2019 and showed him channeling something within the house, which he ultimately attributed to the effects of the black smoke.

In the interview I conducted in July, this is what he shared:

The House on Round Top Farm, aka The Conjuring *House, in Harrisville, Rhode Island. (Photo Courtesy of Julie Griffin)*

Carl Johnson Phone Interview

July 28, 2019

Carl: It was up on the second floor of the farmhouse on Round Top Road, they call it Round Top Farm now.

It was August 1973, and I was a member of a group based in Rhode Island called PIRO, Parapsychology Investigative Research Organization, and we made a visitation there at the homeowner's request. Carolyn Perron requested we come over and assess the activity there.

While we were conducting the interview process, I heard moving around upstairs, which I had heard when we were there three days prior that turned out to be a painting that propelled off the wall.

So, I made my way upstairs and asked, "What's that noise? Do you have company?"

The Perron daughters said, "Oh no, we hear that almost every day. No, there's nobody up there."

So, I went upstairs. I remember going up the stairs and turning to my left looking in one of the bedrooms, and I saw coming from it smoke rolling down the hallway. It was the oddest thing. This was coming right at me. It wasn't in the form of a human; it was rather amorphous. It came down the hallway – it's a rather small hallway – between the bedrooms, and I was waiting to smell smoke. That's how definite this thing was. It wasn't an impression. I thought there was a fire in the house. I closed my eyes, but it was gone as soon as it reached me. Any smoke, any fog wouldn't have dissipated that quickly. It was just instantaneous. It was gone.

And I'll tell you, there's an update. The shadow ghost is still there. The homeowner, Cory Heinzen, and filmmaker Bill Brock who has been staying there, they've told me repeatedly that every time I come there, activity kicks up after I've left. And something happened when I was there four days ago. All I can think of, and I don't mean to flatter myself, but it remembers me from all those years ago.

Upstairs area of the farmhouse where the black smoke has been seen.
(Photo courtesy of Carl Johnson)

We didn't do anything out of the ordinary while we were there [in 1973]. We were just investigating. So, things have happened after I've been there. I think there's a resonance. I think a responsive chord was struck all those years ago.

Mike: I believe time works differently in that realm, so even though it's been 46 years, maybe to whatever is there it's just like yesterday or last week.

Carl: Yeah, in that realm time is not the same thing, anyway. We could go back and forth on this and get into quantum mechanics.

Elise [Giammarco Carlson] has been doing historical research on this, and I was over there [at the house] with Elise and [researcher and author] Jeff Belanger. We were discussing the house's history, and that's when Cory and Bill mentioned the shadowy presence – smoke – nobody knows quite what to call it. Nobody is saying "shadow ghost," but it's definitely some form of shadow entity. It has its own volition; it seems to know what it's doing. It seems to show up at opportune times.

My other experiences with shadow ghosts include Slater Mill, and what's interesting about the shadow ghost there is people aren't seeing it throughout the three buildings. They're seeing it in one location, the Wilkinson building.

I've seen spikes fly off the blacksmith's bench there, I've seen shadow ghosts, I've seen women come out of the waterwheel pit with scratches on their skin, abrasions. I have seen the shadow ghost twice at Wilkinson Mill, and I consider myself very fortunate.

Mike: That's another one that shows up like the smoke, right?

Carl: In the downstairs it did, but upstairs it was in the form of a man, vaguely anthropomorphic. I can't say it was a full articulated shadow image, but it looked more in human form at that stage. But it was flipping in and out of reality.

As I entered the building with Jeremiah Ouelette that night, the co-founder and director of Investigators of the Unknown, we heard a terrific crash. It sounded like a big partition or panel had fallen. We didn't find anything, but we had been there about 20 minutes, people had gone outside, and I said, "Jerry, one of your people are still up here."

He said, "No, they're all outside."

Shadow man at Slater Mill. (Photo Courtesy of Carl Johnson)

And we looked, and Jeremiah and I both saw it in between two of the antique machines. I want to say it looked like a person, and it was moving very fast and very erratically, not natural motion. People don't move like that.

I went for my flashlight and then it faded away. Then it came back and we were looking at it for a few more seconds, and then it left. It must have known there was something to it.

The second time I saw the shadow ghost there it was down in the waterwheel pit the last Saturday in October before Halloween. I had a few people downstairs who were going building-to-building. There's a fissure in the old wood door, and there was some sort of lighting that looked like a strobe on and off through the fissure. We could see something was going in front of the door to occlude the light, a swarm that had enough substance.

Black mist forming at Slater Mill. (Photo Courtesy of Carl Johnson)

Mike: Do you want to comment about your theories as to what the smoke may have been?

Carl: I would use the terms resonance and *ultra-terrestrial*, very different from extraterrestrial. My theory is these personalities, if you will, can imprint themselves by their own choice, and can imprint themselves on the very material of a building, like infusing memory on a computer chip. It's what we call the *holographic universe*.

The memory is there. They're probably two dimensional, and we perceive these manifestations as three dimensional. And for certain circumstances which we don't fully understand, if we understand them at all, these are projected, and then we have the ghosts. I think memories, with time and strong emotion actually do become encoded in the materials from which a building is composed. And that's where they live, that's where they reside, and they are just activated under special circumstances.

So, I don't think they're coming up from Hell, I don't think they're summoned in a séance, I think they're just part of the fabric of the building. That's why old buildings are more prevalent to hauntings. And, perhaps, there's some lime and quartz deposits in the soil underneath the house. Those secure those impressions, and then they generate, like a battery.

And these dimensional plates are in flux, they move about, they're not static. Sometimes they collide with each other. Sometimes they're in the right place and they project the ghosts. I think that's where the shadow ghost came from that I saw.

And people are seeing it now. Now, to me, Mike, that is the most remarkable thing. I thought this was all before, but that shadowy presence is still there in the house on Round Top Hill. It's still showing itself. I think that's the best it can do. I don't think it can present itself as a solid-looking person, so it comes up with this shadow form. This is something that's part and parcel of the house. And believe me, that is to my surprise that it's still there.

I think they're part of the environment, and I think that's how they maneuver, how they transport themselves. I think sometimes they appear in human form because they're matrixing their environment. They're drawing upon impressions of human beings because we're all over the place, and that would be something to emulate, this structure. But they do it in a distorted fashion. I think their more natural form

Black mist forming at Slater Mill. Subsequent photos showed no mist.
(Photo Courtesy of Carl Johnson)

is formless, smoke and cloud-like.

This theory isn't just original with me. It's also the theory of Lana Brock, my co-author of *Shadow Realms*. They're impressions left behind by once living beings and they slip them on like cloaks. Because they're their own kind of entity they manifest, basically, as human. Now, that is just a guess.

That's why I call them *ultra*-terrestrials. They can look basically like us, but unlike ghosts, human generated spirits, they're not totally replicating as once-living people. They just pull on this human form and can't look like us, except suggestively, which would explain why some of them wear cloaks and hats and seemed dressed. They see humans, they figure that's the way humans dress, so that's what they can pull on and make their way around.

Of course, I could be way off base. We don't know what they really are. Shadow spirits, shadow ghosts, they throw everything we think we know about the paranormal out the window. It's like starting from square one.

What are they? Are they demonic? Are they ghosts? I mean, some kind … they're there. They're more substantial than most ghosts. They seem to have more substance. Shadow ghosts can occlude light. They can walk in front of light. It's almost like the old *Shadow* radio serial, the only thing you can never hide is the shadow.

Mike: [in noir radio show voice] The shadow knows …

Carl: [chuckles] Yeah, they're the absence of light. If you think about it, they seem to be black holes. They're the absence of light and if they pass in front of something, they block it out.

New owners of the House on Round Top Farm, Cory and Jennifer Heinzen, appeared on *The Edge of the Rabbit Hole* livestream show on October 8, 2019, did briefly discuss with us and confirmed the presence of the shadow mist Carl had seen at the house.

According to Cory, "We've had everything from shadow figures, black mists, doors opening and closing. Honestly, it's like everything Andrea has talked about, everything they've experienced. It's just all coming at once. It's coming way too fast, and we haven't even been there four months yet."

Specifically, about the black smoke, Cory stated, "[Bill Brock and I] saw it one night. Then our son saw it on a whole separate occasion, and it was enough for him to say, 'Yeah, I've had enough,' and he went back home. We couldn't get him back down there for about three weeks."

During a follow-up interview on November 5, 2019, with Carl and Keith Johnson following the airing of their return to the farmhouse on the Travel Channel, Keith stated, "I knew there was a very, very vicious, controlling entity in this house. It's the same one I happened to deal with when I was still a teenager the first time I came to that house back in the 1970s. I had to be in the same room with Carl to make sure everything was all right and to pray over him in case things got out of control, which it seemed they were about to at the time."

During the filming of their paranormal investigation, Carl was sitting at a table on the first floor and he suddenly entered some sort of trance-like state in which he kept muttering, "Don't leave … don't leave … don't leave." Carl told us during the November 5 interview, "It wasn't a conscious thought, it wasn't volitional at all, unless it was stemming from my subconscious. I was not willing it. I was letting it speak, whatever it was. When it was saying, 'Don't leave,' it was talking to everyone in the room. In other words, there was a desperation to that cry. … What I was feeling was that it didn't want [us] to leave, it didn't want us to leave the house. … When I got up it was as if I had donated blood or something. You can actually see me staggering when I got out of that room."

When I asked Carl specifically about his comments during the episode about the black smoke, that he had attributed what was happening to this entity, he stated, "I saw this [the black smoke] ushering in just as I had 46 years ago, but not in that room. I had seen it upstairs, originally. It got dark in the room, and I saw it coming around the corner. It actually didn't penetrate the wall, it's like it had to egress to come around the downstairs hallway and go into the room where I was. So, seeing that come in, that was not an

Elise Giammarco Carlson (right) with another examining the upstairs area of the House on Round Top Road where the shadow smoke has been seen. (Photo courtesy of Carl Johnson)

emotional response, except for the sense that, 'Oh, no. Here it is.' It wasn't penetrating my emotional frame. I was actually objectively observing this coming in. My first inclination was, 'Oh, wait 'til I tell these guys I'm seeing this.' And then I thought, 'Oh, no, this sounds too good to be true.' You know, if I come out and say I'm seeing this thing issuing into the room, I don't know if they're going to believe me. I have no corroboration at that point. … That was verified later, because other members of the team did see it, and they did get photographic evidence of it. So, I'm glad I mentioned what I experienced."

It's still unknown who or what this black smoke at the House on Round Top Farm may be. Could it possibly be manifesting there outside the boundaries of time and it actually recognized Carl and Keith from their visits 46 years beforehand as if had just been yesterday since their previous encounter? Why was it asking them to stay, as Carl said, in a cry of desperation? Does this entity, as dark and ominous as it seems, have sensitive emotions?

I had my own interesting experiences at this house while specifically investigating the shadow phenomenon that occurs there during filming for *The Shadow Dimension* in September 2020. Most of the day was spent conducting interviews, but even during those moments strange things occurred. I was in the upstairs bedroom that contains a chalkboard wall and was interviewing Keith Johnson about a bizarre experience he'd had with the exterior window in that room during his first visit to the house with his brother, Carl, in 1973. While I was questioning him, I suddenly began to feel extremely lightheaded and fought hard to prevent myself from rocking backward while I filmed. When Keith finished his story, I closed the camera and sat down on the bed near the interior window for a moment to collect myself. This window had been directly behind me, which is important to note for what happened later. Could this reaction have simply been from stress and fatigue? Perhaps. However, this is the room from which Carl had originally seen the shadow smoke billow up and move out.

Later in the day, Carl and I were conducting an investigation of the middle room upstairs, and the entire room slowly started growing darker. It was extremely gradual, and as it darkened the air grew heavier. The moment we stated we were done, everything instantly lightened back up – the air, the light, everything.

What's even more interesting about this visit is a photograph I took while making a visual sweep of the house. In this photo, the area by the door and the interior window is quite hazy, almost like it's in motion, while the rest of the contents within the room are at a perfect standstill. More intriguing is how the exterior window in the bedroom with the chalkboard, of which most is *not* visible *behind the wall*, is actually seen in almost its entirety within the room, transitioned to the right and covering a significant portion of

Is this energy from a portal around the window and doorway captured on camera? The exterior window in the other room is seen transitioned to the right.

the chalkboard. It looks like some sort of interdimensional phasing was occurring when I captured the photo. Much of our discussion that day centered around Andrea Perron's assertion that the area is a portal cleverly disguised as a farmhouse. Had I captured a photograph of that portal's energy?

While interviewing Andrea for *The Shadow Dimension*, we talked about those rooms, and before I even said anything to her about my experiences in that bedroom which had once been hers, she stated, "You know that [interior] window? I would very often see that very same smoke-like apparition form on the outside of the window beyond that wall in the center bedroom, and then it would seep down behind the window and go through the crack under the door and start to try to manifest in my room. I would say to it, 'You can't come in here right now. I don't know who you are. I'm doing my homework. You're not allowed in here right now. You need to go away.' I was always polite and respectful, but it always did. It would just shapeshift into a smoky haze and then just dissipate through the bottom crack of the door. But that meant it was going into the middle bedroom where I had two sisters that slept that night."

This is an extremely active area of the farmhouse, and now that the home is becoming accessible again, perhaps researchers and investigators can discover answers about these entities and shed some light on the nature of shadowy mists.

Chapter 6

The Wisp

What I call the “black wisp” could probably account for most of the shadow people I’ve ever seen. These are entities that are tall, narrow, very translucent, and very fast. They almost look as if someone hit the fast-forward button on someone wearing dark clothing, and the image moved so fast you could barely see it. However … it was there.

Some of these wisps look as if a human shadow had picked itself off the ground and stood upright, but just for a brief moment in the corner of your eye before it darted away just as soon as you turned to look at it.

I’ve seen a number of these on paranormal investigations over the years, quite more so than any sort of ghostly apparition, but my first encounter was when I was much younger.

The first time I crossed paths with a wisp-type shadow entity was at the house we moved into in Wooster, Ohio, when I was 13 years-old, and it was certainly the most solid of any of the entities I would classify as a wisp. While I was busily unpacking my belongings in my new bedroom, I kept seeing someone standing in the hallway right at my doorway, but each time I would turn to look it would dart away. This being was dark, and like my first shadow person encounter, I couldn't discern any distinguishable features. I could tell it had a head and a body, but that was really about it. It otherwise moved too quickly each time I looked, and while it peaked in my doorway often, I just couldn't make out any other details besides body shape.

This happened numerous times over the first couple months we lived in that house, even after I had finished unpacking my belongings. I finally described what I had seen to my mother and asked her if she had seen something similar. Surprisingly, she said she had. Perhaps, now that I was a few years older and officially a teenager, a young man, she trusted I was old enough for an honest answer about something supernatural within the house, unlike my first experience as a child when I was scared out of my bed and my parents insisted I'd had a bad dream. The way she confirmed my shadow sighting was done quite well – without any concern or alarm in her voice, she simply stated she had also seen it, as if it was no big deal at all. Thus, I wasn't overly concerned about the matter, and I decided to call this fellow "Tom," as in "Peeping Tom."

From that point forward, whenever I would spot this shadow out of the corner of my eye, I would say, "Hi, Tom!" and it would run off. I only got to say this a handful of times, however, since Tom stopped coming around after two or three months. I have no idea where he went, why he left, or why he was even there at the house to begin with.

I decided to chalk up this incident as some supernatural being in the house that was curious about us when we arrived, deemed we were ok after a short duration of time, then went about its business elsewhere or in its own plane of existence. Was he still in the house? I have no idea, but I lived at that house for five years until I graduated high school and enlisted in the Air Force, and I never saw Tom again after those first couple months. My parents continued living there another four years, and I never saw him when I visited, either. Therefore, I also can't say it was a haunted house. It was simply a house which had once seen a short spell of some sort of paranormal activity: a shadow person. A black wisp.

Ironically, when we first moved into that house, there had been a number of tenants in and out of the dwelling in the few years preceding our arrival, and my dad made the remark that if we came home one day and the kitchen chairs were stacked on the table like in the movie *Poltergeist* then we were out of there, immediately. Of course, that never happened and his remarks were meant to be humorous, but something had been there, if ever so briefly.

That wisp shadow entity I experienced at that house seemed to display some sort of intelligence, a curiosity, at least, and the cognizance to know when to turn away and flee. Keith and Sandra Johnson also believe this was the case with a shadow Sandra once witnessed. Keith is the twin brother of Carl Johnson, and like him, is also a demonologist. Keith and Sandra are regularly called upon to assist individuals in dealing with alleged malevolent paranormal phenomena or potential inhuman infestation in their homes and together have over 50 years of experience as paranormal investigators.

Sandra's Story

My second personal encounter with a shadow figure took place in October 2003. Keith and I were staying at a small local bed and breakfast house during a weekend when we were speakers at Ryan Buell's annual UnivCon conference at Penn State. The name of this small, pleasant bed and breakfast was the Yellow House, part of State College, Pennsylvania.

When I had my sighting, it was bright sunshine in the middle of the morning. I was in the kitchen making coffee before we left, when I happened to glance out the window, and I caught a glimpse of what appeared to be a small "shadow entity" flitting about on the back porch. Now, this back porch was contained within the house, with solid walls and a door leading to the back yard. At first, I only glimpsed it for a moment out of the corner of my left eye. I then turned and was able to get a good enough look at it to ascertain that it was definitely not humanoid in form, and that it was no more than perhaps four feet tall. A peculiar sensation came over me immediately after witnessing it, which I can only describe as an almost electrical tingling sensation within my thighs. I'd never experienced a sensation quite like this. As I watched, the shadow figure quickly darted from the porch and dashed across the back yard, finally disappearing behind a small, historic-looking building next door.

The thing is, whenever you hear someone say that they see something out of the corner of their eye, skepticism automatically comes up. However, when you then turn and look straight forward and the thing's still there, you know that it's not a figment of your imagination. It's not some trick of your visual field.

Keith's Take

As Sandra and I discovered shortly before we departed for home, this shadow figure had eclipsed itself into a small historical cemetery, located behind the small historic building next door. According to a local woman who we spoke to, this building had once served as a masonic meeting hall, as well as a church.

It is my personal opinion that the shadow figure Sandra witnessed did possess some level of intelligence, and that it was intentionally showing her where it came from, perhaps even anticipating that she and I would briefly investigate the spot before we left.

I also believe that shadow figures function on an interdimensional level. Sandra believes this as well, and also theorizes that they can be a form of time displacements.

Like I said at the beginning of this chapter, I've seen a number of these wisps on paranormal investigations, each exhibiting similar types of activity, such as peering into a room from outside or blowing right through a room altogether. I saw this a few different times at the Stone Lion Inn in Guthrie, Oklahoma, and on one particular night, saw it several times. It was, perhaps, an overly-charged evening at the mansion that night in comparison to the other nights in which I'd investigated there.

The Stone Lion Inn in Guthrie, Oklahoma.

The Stone Lion Inn is a historic family home, originally built by the Houghton's and served a short time as a mortuary in the 1930s, but now operates as a bed and breakfast and murder mystery dinner theater. To me, the building is the epitome of a haunted house, and I've never been disappointed with activity there. Overall, it has a "creepy cool" ambience about it and some have reported seeing apparitions of a little girl or a man in a top hat there, but most of my experiences there were rather mild. That is, except for the one night …

It started rather innocuously during a routine EMF (electromagnetic field) sweep of the library. This is part of our investigative technique to try to determine whether or not a strong EMF field may be playing into the reported experiences of the household. The library is generally a quieter part of the household in regards to paranormal activity, yet as I neared the ornate fireplace, the meter suddenly surged into the red and a wave of energy swept over me. I felt as if I was about to pass out. However, as quickly as the surge had come, it had gone. What it was I still don't know, but it was just a prelude to the rest of the evening.

There's a bureau resting in the main entrance hall blocking the main double doors to a bedroom for the bed and breakfast that had once been a parlor (now called The Parlor Suite). For some odd reason one of the top drawers of the bureau had been open and it suddenly slammed shut as we gathered near the small hall that now takes you to The Parlor Suite's entrance. We all rushed out to see what had made the noise and noticed the changed state of the drawer.

One of our investigators, Johnny, had his Tri-Field EMF detector out and was busy trying to get a reading while I started snapping away with my camera. While Johnny didn't get a strong reading, I did, in fact, capture a white wisp hanging in the air between Johnny and the bureau.

A white wisp forms between Johnny and the bureau.

A few minutes later we decided it would be best to split into two groups; there simply just wasn't enough room for all of us back in The Parlor Suite. I started leading a team upstairs and was about halfway up when one of our other investigators started to set forth upward after me. Suddenly, a framed photograph on the wall between us fell and shattered across the stairs. We all jumped at the surprising crash. When we caught our breath, we noticed what had fallen was a photograph of Lizzie Borden, the infamous New England spinster who was accused of hatcheting her parents to

The framed photo of Lizzie Borden is seen on the wall before it fell.

death in 1892.

That wasn't the only haunting around the stairs that evening. Later on, a group of us decided to return upstairs after the house had grown abnormally quiet. We all stopped ascending the staircase for a moment when the door to the Lucille Mullhal bedroom suite in front of us creaked open and a glimpse of a shadow seemed to cross through. It was a doorway in which on previous visits to the house we had also seen shadows dart in and out. Was this shadow what had caused the framed photo of Lizzie Borden to crash to the stairs? Was it what had slammed the bureau drawer shut and manifest as a white wisp? Was it also what had blown through me in the library and nearly caused me to pass out? Or were all of these separate entities? Further investigation of the Stone Lion Inn is certainly needed.

The most intriguing of all of these incidents with the shadow wisps also occurred in Oklahoma, in the town of Muskogee at a restaurant called Johnny V's, which is no longer in operation. What happened at Johnny V's Ristorante and Pizzeria has really helped me define what I believe true shadow people to really be.

We were just finishing up our investigation, and I decided I was going to take one last photo sweep of the restaurant. Some of the others from the team were upstairs in the bar area while others were out in the dining room when I waltzed through the main doors of the kitchen with my camera. That's when I saw it.

It was tall, narrow, translucent, and wispy. And it was so damn fast. I couldn't really say it had any significant discernible shape since it couldn't have been any more than six or eight inches wide, perhaps as tall as an average man, but it zipped out of there so quickly it was extremely hard to tell. From straight in front of me as I entered the room, it immediately darted to the right side of the room, and I heard it blow right through the thin, flimsy metal doors in the wall that led to the back part of the dining room. The imperative word is *heard*. The doors didn't actually move at all. What had I just seen?

I called out to the others, "Did you guys hear that?"

"Yeah!"

I questioned them on the incident, even going so far as to ask them if they had thrown something at the door in case they were trying to give me a quick jump scare. Could it have possibly been that those up in the bar, a loft-type area above the kitchen with railings overlooking the restaurant, had tossed something down that would've rattled the door? Or did the two that were out in the dining room, even though they were far in front, launch something across the room that would have slammed against the door? They hadn't, of course, and if they had thrown something at the door, I certainly would have seen it move. Made to be easy to walk in and out of the kitchen while holding large trays of food, the door was so flimsy that just barely touching it with your fingertip would have caused it to open. I certainly would have discovered whatever they may have thrown on the floor outside the door if they had done so, and I ventured through to have a look in case they really had been trying to get me to jump. There was nothing.

The door the shadow sounded like it ran through is on the right.

That the others in the group heard the same as I, it was fantastic to get that sort of confirmation, but I was able to get further confirmation of what I'd heard later when I listened back over the footage from my digital audio recorder which captured the loud banging sound. There it was, loud and clear – *bang!*

The fact that this entity blew through that door in which you could hear the sound of it but you could not see the door physically move is of great significance. There are certain interdimensional factors in this encounter that we will explore deeper in Chapter 17. This was not simply a momentary glimpse of a shadow entity as it may seem on the surface. There are particular clues we can glean from its behavior to help give us a deeper insight into the supernatural world.

Chapter 7

The Crawler

Like something out of a popular horror movie, the crawler is probably the creepiest of all the shadow entities. Humanoid in shape, exceedingly fast in movement, and crawling about like so many possession victims in the latest blockbuster smash film, the crawler shadow entity is certainly a force to be reckoned with. While so many of the other entities I've grown to question over the years as to whether or not it may be nefarious in nature, I've yet to hear one crawler story which had any sort of benign aspect to it. They've all been rather sinister, including my own singular experience.

Black Bear Church is out in the middle of nowhere in Olive Township, Oklahoma, but it is certainly one of the most haunted locations I've ever visited. In the cemetery across the dirt road from where its ruins stand, I captured some of my most distinct electronic voice phenomena (EVP), and along the dirt road that leads into the area I heard some of the most life-like heavy boot steps that never turned out to be human at all. However, it is in the church itself, a former place of worship for the local good-natured folk that farm the area, in which lies something truly dark – the crawler.

The crawler acts exactly as its namesake states – it crawls. Along walls, ceilings, floors, and up staircases, it crawls on all fours with long, spindly arms and legs like a super-charged four-legged spider. In some cases, it's been described as scuttling about like a crab along the floor or even up staircases.

Abandoned Black Bear Church in Olive Township, Oklahoma.

Our experience of the crawler at Black Bear was more of the lanky spider variety, ungodly fast, and menacing. It slinked in through one of the basement windows as we conducted a paranormal investigation there and began to circle us. What started off as some creeping shadow soon became a flurry of arms and legs, so quick that it was almost a blur. Around the ceiling and walls it whirred, at some point hitting the floor and knocking a soda bottle across the room. The entire basement darkened and grew ominous. At one point, it seemed to clang against the metal railing of the stairs that led down to the room, and our audio equipment suffered from an outburst of electric feedback that could not have been caused by anything local – we were literally out in the middle of nowhere.

The basement of Black Bear Church where we experienced the crawler. The soda bottle it kicked is seen near the bottom of the photo.

The psychic with us that evening suggested we start singing hymns to create a more positively charged atmosphere and, hopefully, drive the entity away. This we did, and soon after the crawler slid out through the window from whence it came. This harrowing experience was featured on the *My Ghost Story* episode "Church Of Darkness."

There are many local rumors surrounding this particular crawler, and we were not unfamiliar with them when we visited although we had yet to experience the entity prior to that night. According to legend, after the church had been abandoned and left to ruin, it began being frequented by local teens and others as a place to hang out and party (this is absolutely true given the amount of graffiti along the walls and empty beer cans strewn about). One of these groups were associated with some sort of cult who would perform rituals within the confines of the church. During one particular ceremony, they successfully summoned a demon – the crawler – and from that time forward this crawler made the church building its home, defiling a former house of God. Flocking to this creature were many minions, shorter shadow entities who could not cross the threshold of the sanctuary but remained lurking outside, protecting the crawler and its new domicile.

There is no way to know for sure if any sort of group performing occult rituals ever set foot inside the church. I must take a moment to clarify that it was *after* the church became abandoned that these practices are said to have taken place. When attempting to film at the church for the *My Ghost Story* episode, the owner of the property mistook what I said in my short YouTube documentary on the hauntings of Black Bear Church and thought I stated the parishioners of the church were the ones who performed the rituals. This was not the case, but the misunderstanding kept us barred from filming the recreations for the episode at the abandoned church and we used the basement of the Great White House of the historic 101 Ranch instead (thank you 101 Ranch Old Timer's Association).

In any case, there is no way to prove whether or not this summoning really occurred since none of us were there when this supposedly happened. However, it is interesting to note that in one of the back rooms of the church is a concrete slab on top of a brick pedestal in which we had found scorch marks and once the charred bones of some sort of animal. If there was someone who tried performing some sort of ritual of black magick there then this *may* be the place it was performed, but again, there's no way to know for sure. One could interpret that as evidence of a summoning just as well as someone could have created a flame there to reheat a drumstick of fried chicken. We can't just jump to a conclusion because it fits the story we want to tell. Still … there is a crawler who lurks at the old church. We've experienced the frantic whirlwind of its presence.

The pedestal in which we found possible evidence of occult ritual work.

I've been asked several times about the growing number of crawler reports and if crawler activity is increasing nationwide. Some seem to think that with the growing number of reports there must be some sort of plot being hatched from wherever they come to infiltrate our plane of existence and increase supernatural terrorism around the world, particularly in the United States. I've been asked the same about black-eyed children with the same type of premise in mind – reports are growing, there must be a plot – so, although they're two completely different types of entities, I'll address both with the same answer.

Yes, reports of crawler activity seem to be increasing. One

rarely heard about crawlers twenty or thirty years ago, but now there seems to be a bevy of stories concerning these beings. The same is true of BEKs. However, a lot has changed in the world over the past twenty to thirty years.

First and foremost, there are more people in the world these days than there were back then. As population grows, so do the raw numbers of anything that is reported. Statisticians use that fact to their advantage all the time. The raw number of something may go up (perhaps murder), but in reality, the percentage per capita may actually go down if the population also received a large increase. Depending on who they're trying to persuade to a certain point of view, they may use one or the other perspective to say it's gone up or down. Thus, just given the fact there are more people in the world, there are, naturally, going to be more reports of these types of entities.

Secondly, people are more willing to come forth with their stories these days. One of the strong positives that has come out of the plethora of paranormal television shows that have graced our sets since *Scariest Places On Earth* premiered in 2000 is that our current popular culture has made people more comfortable to come forward with their tales of paranormal encounters. It used to be if you talked to someone about seeing a ghost or mentioned you lived in a haunted house you would be laughed at and ridiculed. Some communities would completely cut you off and accuse you of practicing some sort of devilry. There are still pockets of this today, but it's nowhere near as bad as it had once been. Those early pioneers who shared their experiences, even as far back as Harry Price and Hans Holzer, have made it possible for people to let the world know what kind of activity is really going on in the supernatural realm. Again, this means that as we get more comfortable in sharing our experiences, more experiences with crawlers will come forth.

Thirdly, and it's related to the second, it becomes easier for one to share his or her story when someone else has already gone ahead and shared their own experience. In other words, it's harder to be that first person to come forth and claim to have seen a creepy shadow creature crawling along the ceiling on all fours like a crab than it is the hundredth. It feels more comfortable coming out with your story when you already know there are many others who have experienced the same than the first few people who risk ridicule, scorn, and public backlash. (This is actually the premise for our *Encounters With The Paranormal* book series – people sharing in their paranormal experiences to help each other realize they're not alone in all of this.)

Over the past couple years, prior to the writing of this book, I've had private homeowners contact me about crawlers in their homes, particularly crab-like ones creeping up their stairs, and I was there the day after a reported crawler sighting in the psychiatric ward of the abandoned, and now razed, St. Joseph's Hospital in Lorain, Ohio, a menace which was said to have first emerged as a seemingly humanoid-type shadow person in the hallway, then dropped down to all fours and scampered after the investigators who were present. Although I'd been in the psychiatric ward many times and never experienced this phenomenon, this encounter happened a week after an initial sighting of the entity by Eclipse Paranormal. In those particular cases, I did not witness these crawlers. The one at Black Bear Church remains the only one of this type of shadow entity I've seen to date, but it's fair to say that people have become more comfortable over the years in reporting the strange and unusual paranormal activity they've witnessed.

PART II

Just A Dream?

It's a place where you will learn
To face your fears, retrace the years
And ride the whims of your mind
Commanding in another world
Suddenly, you hear and see
This magic new dimension

—Queensrÿche, "Silent Lucidity"

Chapter 8

Sleep Paralysis

Sleep paralysis is a real biological phenomenon. Shadow people are a real supernatural phenomenon. And sometimes, these two are linked together. Are the shadow people creating the paralysis or are shadow people just a hallucination while your body is still in a state between waking and sleep?

I've experienced both phenomena in what has probably become the biggest lightning rod topic concerning shadow people. The moment a shadow person story starts with the three words, "I woke up," the general medical community shuts down the entire incident as a hallucination in connection with sleep paralysis. So, let's take a look at both.

First of all, what is *sleep paralysis*? The Merriam-Webster dictionary simply defines sleep paralysis as, "a complete temporary paralysis occurring in connection with sleep and especially upon waking." The U.S. National Institutes of Health's National Library of Medicine (NIH/NLM) takes this a bit further. In "Sleep Paralysis, a Medical Condition with a Diverse Cultural Interpretation" available on the NIH/NLM website, the authors state, "Sleep paralysis (SP) is a state associated with the inability to move that occurs when an individual is about sleeping or just waking. It could occur in healthy individuals as isolated SP. It has also been linked with other underlying psychiatry, familial, and sleep disorders. Statistics show that 8% of the general population suffers from SP. Although this value has been described inaccurately, there is no standard definition or etiology to diagnose SP."

Medically, "The phenomenon of a dream happens in the REM phase of sleep, where there is no motion or muscle activity. We tend to have our most emotional dreams during REM sleep, and to stop us from acting out these dreams, the brain keeps us temporarily paralyzed. This paralysis (postural atonia) is as a result of the suppression of the skeletal muscle tone by the pons and the ventromedial medulla, effected by the neurotransmitters γ-Aminobutyric acid and glycine which inhibits the motor neurons in the spinal cord. A serious condition where we start to wake up mentally and become aware while still under REM paralysis is termed SP."

I find it interesting that the above definition actually states within it that there is "no standard definition or etiology to diagnose [sleep paralysis]," essentially cutting the legs out from under the rest of the abstract, but it's still an interesting read as the authors did study the phenomenon within various cultures.

Specifically, regarding shadow people, the NIH/NLM article continues, "The parietal lobe functions in sensation and perception and integrating sensory inputs to the visual system. The parietal lobe is likely to play a role in the intruder hallucinations, especially the superior parietal lobule. Pathophysiology of REM sleep disorders is due to flawed brainstem structures. In SP, the intruder (sense of a stranger in the room accompanied by fear), the increased awareness for a sense of threat or danger is due to the brainstem activation of the amygdala."

That's very technical in nature, of course, but cutting to the chase, it essentially says, "Since your mind is still in a type of sleep state, shadow people are just hallucinations."

And herein lies the biggest issue I have with the medical community's stance on this type of phenomena. If shadow people are simply just hallucinations out of our dreams, then why don't we ever see other things from our dreams morph into our rooms at night? In my dreams, I've been in cars, on boats, in spaceships, yet I've never seen one of those in my room at night. I've never seen a tree or an alligator or a squirrel lurking about in the shadows as my eyes flutter open. I've had dreams in which I've been playing baseball at Fenway Park, yet I've never once seen a giant scoreboard or the famous Green Monster wall or the Pesky Pole in my room. Likewise, I've had dreams in which I'm onstage with Mötley Crüe, yet there have never been pyrotechnics erupting in my bedroom, no crowd cheering and singing to the music, no guitars or drumkits or fire bursting out of Nikki Sixx's bass – for all the fun *that* would be, it has never happened. Nor, has it happened to others.

It's always a shadow person.

Sometimes, it's shadow *people*.

Conversely, many people experience shadow entities while they're wide awake doing other activities. Most of the shadow stories I've already shared in this book have had nothing to do with sleep, and all but one of my own experiences occurred outside the bed. Thus, witnessing a shadow person isn't restricted to a sleep paralysis incident in the middle of the night in one's own bedroom. There are a variety of situations and locations – really, an endless stream – in which an encounter can occur. Don't let that thought frighten you. Not all shadow people are evil as some people and Hollywood would like you to believe (we'll get to that in Chapter 21).

Let me back up a bit here. I'm not here to claim that sleep paralysis doesn't exist. It most certainly does, and I've experienced that very phenomenon. Shadow people also exist. Yet, these two phenomena don't have to – and they don't usually – happen simultaneously. Of course, these are two things that *can* happen at the same time. Just like walking down the street and rain are two different things, yet I could suddenly find myself wet because I'm walking down the street and it suddenly starts raining.

So, why are there so many reports of shadow people while people are in the middle of experiencing sleep paralysis? Perhaps, we're overlooking the simplest of explanations. Perhaps, while we're asleep we suddenly sense that someone else is in the room – anyone who is a parent has experienced this with a child who approaches the bed in the middle of the night. My son, Cameron, was notorious for this. Having had a bad dream or needing a glass of water, instead of tapping me on the shoulder to wake me in the dead of the night, he would just stand at the side of the bed next to me and do … nothing. His *presence* would wake me. How does that work?

The human body emanates a toroidal field of energy outward from itself that is felt by other people nearby and is actually measurable. According to the HeartMath Institute in their published body of academic research, *Science of the Heart*, "The heart's magnetic field, which is the strongest rhythmic field produced by the human body, not only envelops every cell of the body, but also extends out in all directions into the space around us. The heart's magnetic field can be measured several feet away from the body by sensitive magnetometers. … Every cell in our bodies is bathed in an external and internal environment of fluctuating invisible magnetic forces. … These same rhythmic patterns also can transmit emotional information via the electromagnetic field into the environment, which can be detected by others and processed in the same manner as internally generated signals."

The HeartMath Institute's biomagnetic communication research also included studies between humans and animals,

A person's toroidal field of energy can be felt from several feet away. Do you sense a presence in The Force?

noting, "We also have found that a type of heart-rhythm synchronization can occur in interactions between people and their pets."

So, as we're suddenly waking in the middle of the night, some of us are still paralyzed … and then we see the presence of what actually woke us. And this time, it's not our child, or our cat, or the neighbor slamming their car door in the middle of the night. It's a *shadow person.*

Night Terrors

I wanted to take a brief moment to address night terrors since this sleep disorder is often asked about when the conversation turns to shadow people and sleep paralysis. Sometimes, a simple statement is made by a participant in the conversation in which he or she states, "I suffered from night terrors as a child," as if this this should be considered as a shadow person experience.

Night terrors *are* a legitimate sleep disorder in which the sufferer screams and thrashes in his or her sleep, but this phenomenon often gets confused with normal nightmares and even shadow people experiences. However, a person who suffers from night terrors generally doesn't even remember what the terror had been.

In a strange dream I had during the course of this writing, I was driving down a country road and I was being passed by a trio of colorful cars. After they passed me and pulled in front, they did the oddest thing. They started circling each other in the lane. I passed them wondering what in the world was going on when another set of colorful cars did the same thing. Honestly, they could have been the same ones, but I seemed to feel this was a second set. Again, I passed them, but up ahead there was a man walking up the middle of the road. I was in the left lane after passing the strange cars, and I stopped to talk to the man, thinking for some reason he might know what was going on. I rolled down the passenger side window and leaned across to talk to him, but the question never rolled off my tongue.

He was a medium-built man with dark, white-flecked hair and a matching goatee, and dark-complected skin. Mediterranean, perhaps? He looked similar to other men I'd met before, but where he was different was in the seditious smile that broadened across his face. That evil grin caused his eyes to sparkle with malice and the promise of something sinister. Before I could back away, he grabbed my hand so fast I never even saw it happen, and suddenly my hand was pinned to the open window frame in a vice grip I could not get out of. I glanced back up the road and saw the cars speeding our way. I was in mortal peril.

I screamed for help. It was a forced scream. It was as if my body simply didn't want to expel any sort of sound. But I would make it do so. Someone had to be nearby that could hear my cry and get me out of this grip and out of the car before whatever was about to happen would happen. I screamed again.

That's when I heard the voice: "Mike." It didn't come from within the environment, the car, or the roadside. It came from somewhere external. It hit me that it was a woman's voice – my girlfriend at the time – and in that moment I realized I was actually dreaming. It wasn't real. The man with the evil grin disappeared, as did the cars racing toward me. However, the dream world didn't completely collapse. I was still trapped in the car, paralyzed there with my hand still stuck to the window frame on the passenger's side of the car. It was as if the moment in the dream had been completely frozen in time, less the people, and my eyes could at least move to survey the scene. Everything else was in suspended animation, a type of strange sleep paralysis within the dream itself.

It seemed like it had been several moments from the time I'd first started yelling for help, but my girlfriend told me that it had really only been a couple seconds when I finally woke up. Time itself even seemed to work differently in this unusual dream experience. The other unusual aspect of this episode was that while my cry for help in the real world was not enunciated very well (I had screamed from out of my dream through sleep paralysis), there were other things my former girlfriend told me I'd said that she couldn't understand because of the awkward way I was speaking. What's strange about that is in the dream world, after I started shouting for help, that is all I said was, "Help!" So, what these other words she heard me say were and where they came from, I have no idea.

All of this, however – the man with the sinister smile, the sleep paralysis, screaming out in my sleep – does not actually equate to an episode of night terrors.

According to HealthLine, "Night terrors are a form of sleep disorder in which a person partially awakens from sleep in a state of terrors. A sufferer of night terrors experiences an activation of his or her fight-or-flight systems. Night terrors are not nightmares, which are a form of dreaming. Because the person may still be partially asleep during a night terror, they can be inconsolable and unaware of their surroundings. They may have no memory of the episode when they awaken."

Here's the thing ... night terrors are a sleeping phenomenon while shadow people are a waking one. We're not sure what it is the sufferer is experiencing when they're having an episode, and they don't usually even remember when they wake up. Is it possible a shadow person, such as a hat man feeding off fear, is the cause of the night terrors? It's possible, although there's not really a way to know for sure unless a third party is in the room observing the shadow person. It could simply be biological, or if it is supernatural, it may be some other type of entity entirely.

Over the next several chapters we're going to break all of this down and see if we can make some sense out of this type of phenomena between sleep paralysis and shadow people. We'll start at the beginning. Literally.

Chapter 9

Shadow People Throughout World History

The term "shadow people" historically predates the modern internet sensationalism of these entities, predates the 1969 book *The Shadow People* by Margaret St. Clair, and predates other artwork, short stories, folklore, and real accounts of shadow entities over the last 100 years. Shadows are not new phenomena. This kind of activity has been occurring for millennia, and it may only seem recent or has been reported more often of late because of how connected we've become since the advent of the internet. When the world wide web was starting to take off in the mid-1990s, scores of people, including myself, started connecting with other experiencers of supernatural activity on forums, groups, and online boards, finally realizing there were many, many others who had experienced the same type of phenomena. We were *not* alone.

Once paranormal and supernatural television shows became en vogue, these numbers skyrocketed as more and more people felt free to talk about the strange things they had seen. No longer was it taboo to talk about shadows, ghosts, and aliens. No longer were you going to find yourself locked away in a straitjacket for admitting to hearing voices, or seeing shadows move, or having a conversation with the apparition of deceased Aunt Edna at the end of your bed one night. Now, paranormal activity was everywhere. So, naturally, it *seems* like a recent increase of this type of phenomena or even new phenomena starting to occur. But really, it's always been with us.

Madame d'Espererance, 1855 - 1919

"Shadow people" is not a modern term but has been mainstream since as far back as the spiritualism movement of the 1800s. Controversial English medium Madame d'Esperance frequently told of her experiences growing up in a haunted house in the 1860s and how she was actually protected from ghosts by shadows, stating, "I was horridly afraid of ghosts. I didn't know what they were, but all the same, I was afraid of them; afraid to move from one room to another without my shadow friends for company."

Hers was another interesting case in which the shadow entities she experienced as a child actually had benevolent qualities to them and served as protectors to her. However, Madame d'Esperance's opinion of shadow people changed as a young adult, [illegible] propensities, was accepted as the probable explanation of the otherwise mysterious occurrence."

The Shadow People Again.

"Some years later, when I had exchanged the busy, occupied life of eldest daughter in a large family for that of a young wife who for several hours a day was left to her own company, I was horrified to find the shadow people reappear, and I began to be tormented by the old fear of a diseased brain. I never spoke of these strange visions, I was too much afraid of people thinking me mad; but the weary secret was a torture to me."

Then Madame D'Esperance began to hear about spiritualism. She scoffed at first, but was soon convinced, and a great peace and rest came to her. She got automatic writing and then she began to sketch the portraits of the shadow people.

"These were generally done in the dark, as I found that the darkness acted as a background, throwing into strong relief every small detail of the figure I tried to sketch. At first I was as much surprised as anybody to find I had actually succeeded in making a tolerably accurate drawing under such conditions. I did not understand how I did it; all I knew was that to me it was not dark. Most of the portraits so drawn were identified and claimed by the friends of the portrayed person, so that out of some hundreds

"A Medium's History" from The Hampshire Telegraph, *Feb. 27, 1897*

as she described, "Some years later, when I had exchanged the busy, occupied life of eldest daughter in a large family for that of a young wife for who several hours a day was left to her own company, I was horrified to find the shadow people reappear, and I began to be tormented by the fear of a diseased brain. I never spoke of these strange visions. I was too much afraid of people thinking me mad."

In Chapter 21 we'll discuss whether or not all shadow entities are evil, but as we can see here, the renowned medium experienced two different types of shadow phenomenon in her life. As a child, she experienced shadows that protected her from other supernatural entities in her household – perhaps these shadows were the spirits of relatives – but as an adult she experienced shadows that tormented her. Purpose is really individual to each shadow person.

While some of Madame d'Esperance's seances as a medium may have been highly controversial, the shadow people she witnessed were seldom disputed since, well … many others had also witnessed shadow entities in their own lives, no matter the specific vocabulary term they actually used, as we'll see below.

One of the more interesting discoveries throughout my research of this subject is how cross-cultural the phenomena of shadow people really are. For thousands of years, cultures from all over the world not connected to each other have been reporting shadow people, old hag, and sleep paralysis experiences. These sightings have *not* been relegated to one specific region of the globe or one specific period of time. They have been recorded for all time, everywhere.

Perhaps the earliest recording of shadow person activity comes in the form of a Sumerian demon named *Alû*. Alû has no visible features – no mouth, no lips, no ears – it doesn't even have limbs, yet it terrorizes people at night as it hovers over them. In a description that resembles sleep paralysis, it binds the victim's body, including his or her tongue, with the intent to take possession.

In his book, *The Mythology Of All Races Semitic* in 1916, Assyriologist Stephen Herbert Langdon cited a translation of a cuneiform script by Major-General Sir H.C. Rawlinson, from v Pl. 50, A, line 42:

Whom in his bed the wicked Alû covered,
Whom the wicked ghost by night overwhelmed.

According to ancient Akkadian and Sumerian mythology, Alû is supposed to be a vengeful spirit of the Udug (later Utukku), an ambiguous class of demons that were sometimes thought of as good and sometimes as evil. A "good" demon may seem a rather strange concept in our modern culture, but in ancient times a "good udug" would sometimes be invoked against an "evil udug." These invocations were used as a type of medical treatment since many illnesses, diseases, and afflictions were considered demonic in nature and attributed to the "hand of a ghost."

The wicked Utukku who slays man alive on the plain.
The wicked Alû who covers (man) like a garment.
The wicked Etimmu, the wicked Gallû, who bind the body.

The Lamme (Lamashtu), the Lammea (Labasu), who cause disease in the body.
The Lilû who wanders in the plain.

We could get lost in ancient mythology for a while with its vast richness and countless legends, but the point is that even in the cradle of civilization thousands of years ago the phenomena that we now call "shadow people" or "old hag syndrome" absolutely existed. Langdon also tells us in his text that, "Alu can be identified with Ailo, one of the names of Lilith in Jewish demonology."

In Jewish mythology, Lilith is said to be the first wife of Adam, created at the same time and from the same clay as Adam, who refused to take a submissive role and left the Garden of Eden. She has been characterized as the Queen of Demons, perhaps unjustly, but there are many variations to the story. Through these accounts, one could already start tracing lines from Lilith and the fall of humankind to the shadow people we experience today.

Another one of the earliest recordings of shadow entities comes from the ancient Egyptian *khaibit*, one of the seven parts of a person's soul. This part of the soul was considered "the shadow," the piece that remained here on earth in hidden places after a person's death.

Ancient Egyptian beliefs about the human soul are extremely extensive since, according to Sir E.A. Wallis Budge, the former Keeper of Egyptian Antiquities at the British Museum, the Egyptians believed humans had more than one soul. These souls were all separate from each other and had different functions, but they were all connected to the human body, or *khat*.

At death, the spiritual aspect of these souls ascends to the stars to begin the next stage of its journey in the constellation of Orion, but the animating force behind the body is said to remain on earth with the corpse. This force is supposed to be a combination of the *ka* ("double") and *khaibit* ("shadow"). One can already start to see the supernatural implications of parts of a soul being left behind on Earth to roam.

From the tomb of Irinufer in the Theban Necropolis in Egypt, Ba birds with the Khaibit.

From the *Book of What is in the Duat* or the *Amduat*, one of the ancient Egyptian funerary texts:

> *Let thy soul be in heaven ... let thy shadow penetrate the hidden place, and let thy body be to earth.*

Across the globe, ancient Native American cultures also believed in similar concepts of multiple souls, including a shadow-based soul. Investigative journalist, lecturer, and best-selling author on ancient civilizations Graham Hancock reports about several of these in his book *America Before: The Key To Earth's Lost Civilization*:

"In other accounts gathered from among the widely spread Ojibwa people of northeastern North America, the ethnographer

Vernon Kinietz was told that humans have seven souls – only one of which, 'the real soul,' goes to the realm of the dead. Another Ojibwas group reported that, according to their traditions, the human being consists of three parts:

> The body (*wiyo*), which decays after death, the soul (*udjitchog*), which at death departs for the realm of the dead in the West, and the shadow (*udjibbom*), which after death becomes a grave-ghost.

Expressing the same idea in a slightly different way, the Menominee of Wisconsin say there are two souls in every human being:

> One, which is called "a shade across," resides in the head and is the intellect; after death it becomes a grave ghost. The other is the real soul, *tcebai*, which has its seat in the heart and at death betakes itself to the realm of the dead.

For the Choctaw, also, humans have two souls – the *shilombish*, "the outside shadow," and the *shilup*, "the inside shadow," or ghost, which at death goes to the land of the ghosts. The *shilombish* remains on earth."

The ancient Egyptians and ancient Native Americans aren't the only ones who had similar beliefs concerning the shadow realm. Scores of cultures from all over the world have had similar beliefs in a shadow-related phenomenon known as *Old Hag Syndrome*.

Old Hag Syndrome occurs when one wakes in the night to the visage of an old woman or a ghoul sitting on his or her chest. There is a degree of sleep paralysis associated with this phenomenon in that the victim feels as if the entity is pressing down on his or her chest, creating at least partial, and in many cases, complete paralysis. It is from this which originates the term "hag ridden," the disheveled state of a person waking in the morning after a restless sleep and feeling more exhausted than when he or she first lied down. Imagine feeling hung over in the morning when not having a drop to drink the night before.

The Nightmare*, painted in 1781 by Henry Fuseli*

"Hag riding" was also a term used in more contemporary times, but still as far back as the 1700s to describe men being visited by horses or hags while they slept alone, according to old Germanic tales regarding demons and witches during the night. Women were said, in these cases, to engage in sexual encounters with the devil or an *incubus*, a male demon who rapes sleeping women (the converse female is *succubus*).

In 1782, Henry Fuseli revealed his famous oil painting *The Nightmare*, which depicts a sleeping woman stretched out with an incubus or ghoul sitting on her chest while a black horse looks on. It's believed Fuseli suffered from "waking nightmares" in which he experienced something similar to the old hag, but it was also rumored he ate pork before going to bed in order to stimulate his dark dreams. It's difficult to know the truth of the matter, but Fuseli would go on to paint and draw multiple variations of *The Nightmare* for the next 15 years.

In 1783, an engraving of *The Nightmare* created by Thomas Burke began circulating, and it included the following short poem by Erasmus Darwin, titled "Night-mare":

So on his Nightmare through the evening fog
Flits the squab Fiend o'er fen, and lake, and bog;
Seeks some love-wilder'd maid with sleep oppress'd,
Alights, and grinning sits upon her breast.

Who or what this old hag people experience in the depths of the night may really be is largely unknown and widely speculated upon, but it has been represented in artwork and folklore for centuries. The medical community, as noted in the previous chapter, simply says this hag or ghoul is just a hallucination. The following list is a small sample of legends and folklore from around the world concerning the shadow phenomenon known as Old Hag Syndrome, and is by no means all-inclusive. It's just meant to give you an idea of what multiple cultures have had to say about it for millennia.

Pakistan: *Shaitan* – Phenomenon is believed to be caused by an evil djinn or demon who has taken over a person's body.

Persian culture: *Bakhtak* – Ghost-like entity who sits on the chest of a sleeping person.

Turkey: *Karabasan* – The dark presser, a type of evil spirit.

Fiji: *Kana tevoro* – Being eaten by a demon or a recently deceased relative who has returned to complete some unfinished business.

China: *guǐ yā shēn* (鬼壓身/鬼压身) or *guǐ yā chuáng* (鬼壓床/鬼压床) – “ghost pressing on body” or “ghost pressing on bed”

Japan: *Kanashibari* (金縛り) – “bound or fastened to metal”

Ethiopia: *Dukak* – Literally means depression, but also the name of an evil spirit that possesses people during their sleep. *Dukak* is also sometimes the anthropomorphic personification of the depression that may follow after quitting the habit of chewing khat, a native plant with a stimulant that causes euphoria.

Swahili speaking areas of Southeast Africa: *Jinamizi* – “strangled by djinn” or a creature sitting on one’s chest making it difficult to breathe.

Sardinia: *Ammuttadori* – Demon who sits on the chest of a sleeping victim, sometimes ripping the person’s skin off with its nails. Sometimes this demon wears seven red caps on its head, and if the victim manages to steal one of these caps, he or she will find a hidden treasure.

Scandanavian folklore: *Mare* – Evil female entity which rides on people’s chests while they sleep. An alternative, *Mara*, are said to be the souls of damned living women pulled from their bodies at night to ride the chests of other villagers.

Brazil: *Pisadeira* – Tall, skinny old woman with white, tangled hair who steps on the chests of those who sleep with a full stomach.

And on and on …

What I find amazing is that there are so many cultures throughout world history that have reported this phenomenon, most of which had no contact with each other at all, and they all, essentially, deduced the same characteristics about it. And none of them came to the conclusion that it was a hallucination. How is the Brazillian *Pisadeira* so much the same as the Scandanavian *Mare*, which is essentially the description of the Persian *Bakhtak*, if they are not really the same type of entity? Surely, a person in Rio de Janeiro in 1642 wasn't sharing the same hallucination or experiencing group psychosis with a person in Persepolis in 510 BC. That these experiences have happened to individual people for thousands of years in all parts of the world is compelling.

Admittedly, there is some folklore added to those descriptions above of world night hag phenomenon – there always seems to be a little additional storytelling with the ancients – but with the truth engrained in all of these tales, where does the folklore end and the real experiences of shadow entities begin?

CHAPTER 10

EXPERIENCING REAL SLEEP PARALYSIS

Most people tend to experience sleep paralysis as part of a waking phenomenon, and this has happened to me, in part, once. It's happened to me as part of a falling asleep phenomenon twice, and we'll get to that in a moment. The time I experienced sleep paralysis upon waking only my right arm and part of my upper body had actually been paralyzed. This wasn't the classic "arm falling asleep" experience of blood circulation being cut off – I've experienced that countless times – and am very familiar with the "pins and needles" sensation of the blood returning to its normal course throughout my arm. This was just a strange deadening of the arm. I could pick it up and drop it like it was dead weight, and my arm didn't feel a thing. Within moments, I returned to full functionality, but it was an odd experience, and I saw no shadow people.

The two times I experienced sleep paralysis while falling asleep were very similar in nature, both in compromising positions in which I did not want to be falling asleep. Yet, my body was completely exhausted and it shut down on me, leaving me in the remarkable, yet horrific position of being asleep and awake at the same time, completely conscious yet unable to move. On top of it, everything was black. I could not see.

The first time this happened to me I was certainly frightened. I knew my body was asleep, but I had no idea how long I was going to stay locked into place or if I was even going to be able to get out of it at all. The situation involved work – I was at the office – and if I was absent too long (*Was I going to be paralyzed for hours?*) I would certainly get into trouble. Worse yet, I could be discovered in my condition, equally getting into trouble yet having embarrassment lumped on top of it. I could hear voices around me, so the situation was dire. What could I possibly do to get out of my alarming predicament?

Could I wiggle a toe? I thought that if, perhaps, I could at least do that then maybe I'd have a chance. It didn't happen immediately, but after enough sheer will, yes, I could wiggle a toe. Could I wiggle another? Again, with enough sheer will, I was able to do it. And so forth it went, working up my legs to my body to my shoulders and, finally, my head as I willed myself back awake from the horrors of sleep paralysis.

My heart pounded in my chest, and I was amazed at what had happened to me. Was I really so sleep-deprived at the time that my body just instantaneously fell asleep with my mind still conscious? Yes, it really did. My body completely shut down with my mind still fully awake. Thus, I was able to experience true sleep paralysis. Yet, throughout this entire time being stuck in the position I had been, I saw no shadow people.

I certainly wasn't looking for shadow entities at the time. I was a mere 20 years old and didn't know at all yet about the legends and lore or the accounts of other people's experiences surrounding the things I had seen when I was younger. I was very interested in all things supernatural, but information about such things still wasn't as easily accessible as it is today. Similarly, the term "sleep paralysis" didn't become a part of my vocabulary until years later. I was simply scared and trying to exit a serious situation.

The second time this happened to me it was 17 years later, and I wasn't nearly as frightened as I had been the first time around since I'd been through it before. Sure, I was a bit nervous since I found myself in that horrific state once again, and once again, it was in the midst of a work-related situation. But I applied the same principals I had the first time, and I was able to work myself out of the situation in no time. Again, I didn't see any shadow people. By this point in time, I was well-versed in shadow phenomenon and had been giving lectures on the subject. Alas, no shadow being made its presence known this second time either.

In fact, the vast majority of the accounts sent my way over the years concerning sleep paralysis do *not* include shadow people. It is a rare phenomenon, actually, that they do occur together, and it makes me wonder why the medical community is so adamant that shadow people are simply a hallucination occurring during sleep paralysis when these two phenomena occurring together are the exception rather than the norm.

Sometimes, however, these things do occur together and these situations can be very frightening for the person involved. One particular woman who frequents the chat room during our *Edge of the Rabbit Hole* livestream show on Tuesday nights related her personal shadow person sleep paralysis incident during one of our broadcasts. Her handle is LulyTubee.

LulyTubee's Story:

I was taking a nap during the day in my guest room. The curtains were open, so there was plenty of light in the room, and I had fallen asleep on my stomach. A little while later, I woke up in a state of sleep paralysis, and I was only able to move my eyes. I could sense a presence in the room, and I looked over to the TV.

The TV was off, but I could see a presence leaning on his left side on the nearby door frame. He looked to be about six-foot-one or six-foot-two – I'm six feet tall, so I could tell his height. From the doorway, he started walking toward me, and I still couldn't move.

He walked up to my legs, but I could no longer see him. I felt the mattress move as he climbed up on the bed, and as he moved up more on the bed, I could see him again through the reflection of the TV. He then laid on top of me with his full body weight.

I was horrified and passed out praying The Lord's Prayer. It's scary as hell because you cannot move in your most vulnerable state. There's someone or something you don't know in your space touching you. It's the worst. It's happened before, but that particular day I thought I was safe by taking a nap during the day to try to avoid it.

There are a couple interesting takeaways from this story that are different from many others but reinforces the idea that old hag syndrome is real, personal, and individual to the person having the experience. First, the entity involved in this incident was a humanoid figure, not the old hag, some sort of ghoulish creature, or an incubus. Secondly, Luly was on her stomach during this incident. Most people report having this type of experience while on their back, and some skeptics of the phenomenon have theorized that lying on one's back is what helps make one prone to having a combined sleep paralysis and shadow person experience. While terrifying for Luly, this makes her experience rather unique, but I believe most experiences are.

Another interesting shadow person encounter combined with sleep paralysis was conveyed to me at a conference after I showed a woman the humanoid figure illustration from Chapter 1. She fully admitted that she wasn't sure if this experience was a dream or if it was real, however, she awoke lying on her back, which was her norm. Suddenly, she was startled by a flash of light from a room out in the hall. She wasn't sure what this flash was, but a shadow man – she specifically made sure to call it a man – rushed into her room and jumped on top of her. It pinned her down, paralyzing her to the bed, and she then heard laughter. After a brief moment, it jumped off her and ran back into the other room after which she saw another flash of light.

The next day, she entered that room and flipped on the light switch. Two flashes of light burst forth in the room and the smell of burnt electronics filled the air. Most of the electronics in the room had completely fried, and she called the fire department.

Was what she experienced really a dream, perhaps a premonition of what was to come the following day? Was she really visited by a shadow person whose energy from the night before caused the electrical components to destroy themselves the next day? Or was it nothing, perhaps just a power surge when she turned on the light switch, and her perceived experience from the night before was just simply all a coincidence?

I don't believe in coincidences.

Chapter 11

Witnessing Old Hag Syndrome

Paranormal activity is extremely difficult to prove. Most of the field is based purely on theory that is very difficult to substantiate, and even those that investigate "scientifically" with scores of various electronic devices have their work cut out for them since setting up a scientific investigation without a true control object is troublesome. If you're trying to prove a location is haunted, how do you ensure you set up a control object of a location that is *not* haunted to run your tests against both? (Your tests have to become extremely, extremely specific, but most people don't do that.) Similarly, the photographic and audio pieces of evidence that are collected are routinely dismissed by skeptics as "something that could be Photoshopped" or the sound of "clothes moving." So, it helps when more than one person witnesses and experiences the same thing on a paranormal investigation. When more than one person is able to corroborate an incident, it tends to make the story more reliable.

A major obstacle that faces victims of Old Hag Syndrome is that they usually face the hag alone; either they're on their own or the person they're with is fast asleep when the moment occurs. The same is true of those who wake in the middle of the night to a shadow person standing in the corner of their room. It's usually a very solitary moment. Thus, it's extremely easy for the medical community to dismiss the entire incident as simply a hallucination brought on by a lingering sleep state. No one else saw the phenomenon, after all. However, not all incidents of Old Hag Syndrome and sleep paralysis are witnessed alone.

One of the more interesting stories conveyed to me over the years regarding shadow people and the old hag was just recently related to me at a conference in which I was speaking on the subject. I had also already started this manuscript, so its addition midway through the project was extremely timely and welcome. After my presentation, a middle-aged married couple approached me to impart a fascinating story about an encounter in which one partner witnessed the struggles of the other with the old hag. However, this time it wasn't just an old hag – it was a dire wolf.

Julie awoke in the middle of the night one evening pinned to the bed and unable to move with an immense weight upon her chest. She struggled, but couldn't wrench free from whatever was keeping her pressed to the bed. Her eyes adjusted to the dim light, and to her horror, a great dire wolf, fangs bared, lay atop her with its massive paws crushing her shoulders back into the mattress. She struggled against the immense weight and power, but it was no use. She was trapped.

Dan, Julie's husband, was startled awake by his wife's struggles. The room was pitch black, and he could barely see, but he knew his wife was in some sort of trouble, something more than the average bad dream. He rushed to turn on the light and was shocked by what he saw.

Pressed deep into the bed was Julie, wide-eyed and struggling with something unseen. Her body was stiff but jerking as if she was fighting to push something off of her; however, Dan couldn't actually see the massive creature that had pounced on his wife. To his horror, he did see massive indentations pressed into the skin of her shoulders as if enormous invisible paws were keeping her pinned to the mattress.

Suddenly, the wolf leapt away, the indentations disappeared, and Julie, finally free from the creature's grasp, rushed to her husband. They were both terrified, but Julie survived unscathed.

Although he hadn't actually seen the wolf, Dan believed Julie's account of the wolf since he had witnessed the impressions of the giant paws pressed into her shoulders. Since the creature was still invisible to Dan's eyes, some may disregard this story as being a true eyewitness account, but the fact he saw the indentations of the paws on her body makes this a genuinely notable case.

Meghan's Story:

I was dating my ex, another pagan, and his house definitely had some supernatural stuff going on, but I didn't know anything about it until I started getting affected. My ex would leave really early in the morning for work, around 5:00 AM. One morning, after he had left and I was sleeping in until I had to leave by 7:00, I was under the covers and heard the door open and his voice say, "They didn't need me at work, so I came back."

There was something different about his voice, however. I then felt an energy that let me know something was up, but I was kind of in sleep paralysis. The voice then moved around the room and bed and continued to talk to me to try to get me to come out from under the covers. The bed then depressed down next to me as if someone sat on it, which is when I yelled as best I could, "Go away!"

Suddenly, the bed lifted back up, the energy left, and I was able to move and quickly leave the house. I never stayed in his room without him after that.

This same thing occurred several other times at night while I was sleeping next to my ex. Finally, one night I felt like something was right next to me at the bedside. It definitely had a negative feeling, but I was frozen. My ex was sleeping next to me with his arm over me and our hands were clasped together. I did all that I could to shake his arm and moan to get him to wake up, but I was, again, in some sort of sleep paralysis. All of a sudden, he shot up in bed and yelled, "What was that?"

He started moving toward the end of the bed to go after whatever was there, at which time, I was finally able to move and speak freely. I gave him no insight into what I had experienced and felt, but when I asked him what he saw he told me he opened his eyes and saw a large black mass standing next to me. When he reacted and yelled, he saw it move toward the end of the bed and out the window.

It was kind of nice to know that he saw something that I was experiencing without me having to tell him what I was going through. Nice to get some validation. After that he needed to do two cleansings to get rid of whatever it had been, and I never had those experiences again.

What's interesting about Meghan's story is that she's not actually the one who saw the shadow mass. Her ex-boyfriend is the one who saw a black shadow mass hovering near Meghan's side of the bed while she was in the grips of sleep paralysis. He had no idea she had been in that state while she felt something negative by the bedside, yet he saw precisely what that negativity had been.

Sleep paralysis can come in a variety of forms, and for the person witnessing someone else battling this phenomenon, it can be almost as disconcerting and frightening.

In September 1995, while I was still in the U.S. Air Force, I was on a temporary duty assignment with a joint contingent out of Alaska to Ft. Polk, Louisiana. I was excited for this short assignment since my grandfather had been assigned to Ft. Polk for a short time during World War II, and I would be able to visit a close friend of mine who lived in Lafayette. What I didn't expect was to befriend one of the Army personnel for the next 10 days and experience with him, as well as several of the others who were with us, well … what many new 21-year-olds run about and experience. We wreaked havoc at a dive called Spooky's Roost and several of the other hot spots up and down the strip outside Ft. Polk, and earned ourselves the endearing title of "Those Drunk Bastards From Alaska." Although memorable, these were not some of my finer moments, yet during this foray into the depths of Louisiana, a new Army buddy of mine, Jim, related to me a tale just as memorable and quite prevalent to my continuing work long after my military days had ended.

Jim once had a girlfriend who lived with him for a time who had a dreadfully harrowing experience late one night in bed. Jim woke to her writhing in her sleep, locked into place, yet twisting and contorting at the same time. He described it as it looking like the bones were moving inside of her, however, her body remained transfixed into one spot on the bed, paralyzed. He tried to shake her awake, thinking that she may have been having some sort of nightmare, and she did wake … sort of.

Her eyes shot open and her body lurched up. She cursed at him in a deep guttural voice that was not her own and told him he ought to kill himself. Her face was distorted, as if large bones were pushing outward from her skull and stretching the skin.

Jim grabbed her by the shoulders and shouted, "I don't know who or what the fuck you are, but you need to get out of her right now!"

Back and forth they went, Jim yelling, "Get out!" while this thing growled, spat, and yelled obscenities at him. Finally, the entity relented, and the twisted form returned to being his girlfriend. She had absolutely no idea what had happened.

Jim's experience with his former girlfriend isn't really a shadow person encounter, at least it doesn't really seem to be given the information at hand. This story instantly brings to mind a case of demonic possession we've all seen depicted in film. We can't know for sure that this was really demonic — perhaps she was an unsuspecting medium channeling some sort of nefarious and nasty human spirit who took advantage of her in her sleep — but what's always been interesting to me about this story outside of the transformation of the girl's bone structure is the paralysis piece of the tale. As she underwent her exotic transformation she was completely paralyzed in bed. It brings to mind our history study in Chapter 9 and "the dark presser" terminology used by the Turkish culture, the *Karabasan*, in their interpretation of shadow people encounters. So, perhaps, it's related and not biological at all.

There have been a few rare occasions in which I, also, have awoken in the middle of the night to the unnerving sensation that something was pushing down upon me. The force of it was so strong that it was difficult to move, so one might be inclined to say I was experiencing sleep paralysis; however, this felt much different than either of my sleep paralysis moments. In those cases, the sensation was as if I could not feel any part of my body. My mind was aware that my body existed, but there was no physical awareness of my body for me to feel any sort of pressure whatsoever from any direction. It was an unnerving sense of physical nothingness.

In the case of the pressing force, however, I could absolutely feel my body. I just couldn't really move it under the weight of whatever was pushing down upon me. There was an alarming sense that whatever was pressing down upon me wasn't actually trying to crush me; it was trying to *enter* me. It was trying to take over my body for use as its own vessel. Fortunately, it was never successful. Jim's girlfriend, apparently, was not so fortunate, at least for a short period of time.

What I did to block this entity from entering me was I simply prayed. I don't intend to preach any specific religion in this book; that's not what this is about. I'm merely stating what I did in those particular situations, and that is I prayed. My beliefs do not require you to believe what I believe, but I'm confident that if your mind is wholeheartedly set on a particular thing protecting you, whether that is prayer, a talisman, or the ashes of Aunt Jane's cat, then it will protect you.

Of all my own personal experiences I've described in this book, the times I felt like something was trying to enter me were the most frightening. For those that fear the same thing happening to them, take heart — I'm still here to tell the tale. This type of terrifying intrusive phenomenon is something we can battle and withstand.

Chapter 12

Witnessing Shadow People Without Sleep Paralysis

While we've spent the majority of this section of the book dissecting the relationship between sleep paralysis and shadow people, the obvious is staring us right in the face. You don't have to be asleep to see shadow people, and this work is already loaded with scores of accounts of shadow people encounters in which sleep is a nonfactor.

From my personal accounts alone, we've discussed the shadow person I saw outside my bedroom door when I was 13-years-old, the shadow wisp I saw darting across the kitchen at Johnny V's restaurant, shadows darting into the Lucille Mullhal suite at the Stone Lion Inn, the crawler at Black Bear Church, the massive black mist in Talasyn's bedroom in Edmond, Oklahoma, and the shadow person we caught on camera at the Kampsville grade school. For none of these was I actually sleeping or even remotely close to it.

Aside from my own accounts, there are several stories from other people within this tome that recount experiences with shadow people while they have been wide awake. Laurie kept seeing a red-eyed shadow person out her bay window as she walked out of her living room. Tammy Hayn repeatedly witnessed a dark hooded figure drift from her bedroom into her son's room. Cat Gasch was falling down the stairs of an old friary in Ireland when her sister spotted one. Michelle LeBaron was actively investigating the Washoe Club when she saw a hat man. Carl Johnson saw black smoke billow up at him down a hall at the Perron farmhouse. A small group of Tri-C investigators stated a crawler chased them out of the psychiatric ward at St. Joseph's Hospital. And we'll see Brittney Crabb experience a shadow person in the woods in Chapter 14 as well as others who have experienced shadow people outside the confines of their bed.

In no way, shape, or form had sleep been involved with any of these above situations, so my opinion is that the medical community's theory stating shadow people are merely hallucinations within a state of sleep paralysis is completely invalid. It seems to be much more common that shadow people are seen while the observer is awake and conscious instead of asleep and in bed.

That said, if one actually *is* in bed during an encounter, one does not have to be in a state of sleep paralysis in order to see a shadow person. My first shadow person experience was in bed, but I was certainly mobile. My mouth opened wide, my arms moved across my body, and my head turned to the side as the entity ran off down the hall. Shawn Gilmore was able to turn over in bed when he saw a shadow person enter his room and exit through the closet. Tonia was able to scream at her hat man with the cape.

Essentially, there doesn't seem to be any consistent pattern between seeing a shadow person and experiencing sleep paralysis, not even when trying to narrow these situations down to specific types of shadow experiences. Even with Lacye Lembcke's experience with the three hooded figures next to her bed she was able to move her head. Are we to somehow draw conclusions that in specific situations if you're 95% paralyzed then you'll see hooded figures, but if you're 100% paralyzed then a humanoid figure will climb atop you? (This doesn't work anyway since I was 0% paralyzed when I witnessed the humanoid figure while in bed.) Each situation seems to be, well, situational. Thus, we cannot simply lump shadow people, or even specific types of shadow entities experienced, into an effect of sleep paralysis.

But what about Old Hag Syndrome? Surely, with Old Hag Syndrome – the dark presser, the *Karabasan* – a victim must be experiencing sleep paralysis at the time. Luly in Chapter 10 was paralyzed when a dark figure pressed down on top of her and Julie in Chapter 11 was paralyzed while pinned down by the dire wolf.

Actually, it is quite possible to experience Old Hag Syndrome without experiencing sleep paralysis, and paranormal investigator Eric Girard has experienced this type of phenomenon. A native of Woonsocket, Rhode Island, Eric founded Rhode Island Paranormal in 2007, although he had already been investigating supernatural activity for much longer. He recounts his tale of a physical altercation with an entity that may have been the old hag.

Eric's Story:

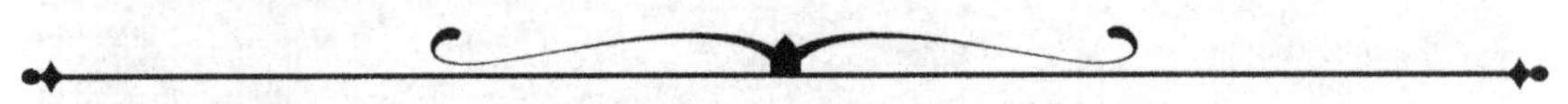

My story took place in September 2015. I had recently separated from my girlfriend who had been living in my house for eight years. My daughter had moved in at this time for three months until she got back on her feet, so I had never slept alone in my house up until my daughter slept at her aunt's house one evening in September.

I went to bed around midnight, and I woke up exactly at 3:00 AM due to a loud thunder crash from a massive storm. I opened my eyes and felt something heavy on my chest. A flash of lightning lit up my room and I witnessed a silhouette of a woman straddling my chest. I was able to view long hair and shoulders but no facial features since the figure and the room were way too dark.

I froze for a split second to make sure I was awake, which I realized I was 100%. I swung my left arm across my chest and grabbed a solid form of a shoulder and pushed it to the left side of my bed. I pushed hard because the figure had weight to it. I ended up rolling right off the bed with this shadow woman still attached to me. I hit the hard wood floor at that time, a lightning flash went off again, and I looked under the bed and saw nothing. I immediately flipped on the lights in the room and found to my surprise that I was all alone!

I ran to the kitchen and grabbed a steak knife and checked to make sure all my doors and windows were locked, which they were. I searched my entire house and found no one else inside with me. I was in complete shock because I knew what I had just seen and felt. This figure was a complete shadow woman with a heavy mass that I was able to touch. I stayed up for two more hours trying to figure out everything that had just transpired. I didn't come to any conclusion at all; I was completely baffled! The next day my daughter noticed three red scratch marks across the lower left side of my back, I didn't even know they were there until she pointed them out.

I would also like to add that not much frightens me at all. I am a 230-pound guy who lifts weights often. I had been a paranormal investigator for 10 years up to that point. I have heard many EVPs, seen objects levitate, and I've witnessed a full body apparition during investigations (and not). I do live in a house with quite a bit of paranormal activity. I have captured voices on recordings that have answered my questions, mimicked my voice, and just plain talking for no reason. My only guess to who this woman may have been is linked to a recording I have of a woman in my home saying, "I love him." She was referring to me at the time, and she had an English accent. I captured her voice back in 2010 along with other EVPs on the same evening. I had in my home along with my girlfriend at the time, Carl L. Johnson, and Dina Palazini. We all witnessed these voices and played them back many times to try and understand their full meaning.

This account is significant for two reasons. For one, it dispels the notion that all Old Hag Syndrome accounts are related to sleep paralysis. While sleep paralysis can certainly occur during instances of Old Hag Syndrome, sleep paralysis does *not* have to be present for the experience to happen.

Secondly, this woman Eric encountered had *mass*. This wasn't some misty apparition or a figment of his imagination. He was able to reach out and physically touch this entity with his own hand, grab it, and push it right off the bed. Where the being went from there, we don't know. Perhaps it scurried away in the blink of an eye, or perhaps it returned to the dimension from whence it came. What's important is that by having a physical form with mass, this entity can help validate for others their own experiences of feeling the weight of someone sitting on their chest, perhaps even seeing them mounted there. Hallucinations don't have mass.

PART III

Deeper Shadows

There's no "supernatural world." Everything that exists is natural.

—Dr. Hans Holzer

Chapter 13

Not Your Typical Ghost

For many years I believed that all shadow entities we witnessed were their own type of supernatural entity. I didn't believe that they could actually be human spirits. However, I harken back to the comment I made in the Introduction of this book: I reserve the right to change my mind. In this particular area of shadow people, I most certainly have changed my mind – not all shadow entities are "shadow people," or what I've now been calling a "true" shadow person. To me, a true shadow person is an interdimensional being, and we'll get to that in Chapter 17, but sometimes, these shadows are simply human spirits. Perhaps, the ancient Egyptians were on to something when they suggested the human soul is separated into multiple parts, and the *khaibit*, the shadow soul, lingers here on Earth.

I was stubborn, but I probably should have taken the hint about the complexity of supernatural shadows and the humanity of some of them in October 2013, at an event called "Tales From The Dearly Departed" at the Montpelier Mansion in Laurel, Maryland. I had been asked to make an appearance at the mansion to read a number of true ghost stories I had written about the Snowden family homes in my book *Ghosts Of Maryland*. The reading was followed by a candlelight ghost tour of the historic home, and we witnessed something that plays right into the history of the mansion.

The estate dates back to the early 1780s, and had the likes of George and Martha Washington, as well as Abigail Adams, spend the night within its walls. With a rich family history, the house is teeming with ghost stories, and the building does not fail to produce paranormal activity. The grand central hall of the mansion has long been said to be haunted by the ghost of an unknown woman floating down the staircase wrapped in a quilt. She may walk through a person, look directly at him or her, and has been seen on several occasions walking through the wall at the lower landing of the staircase which then turns to the hall.

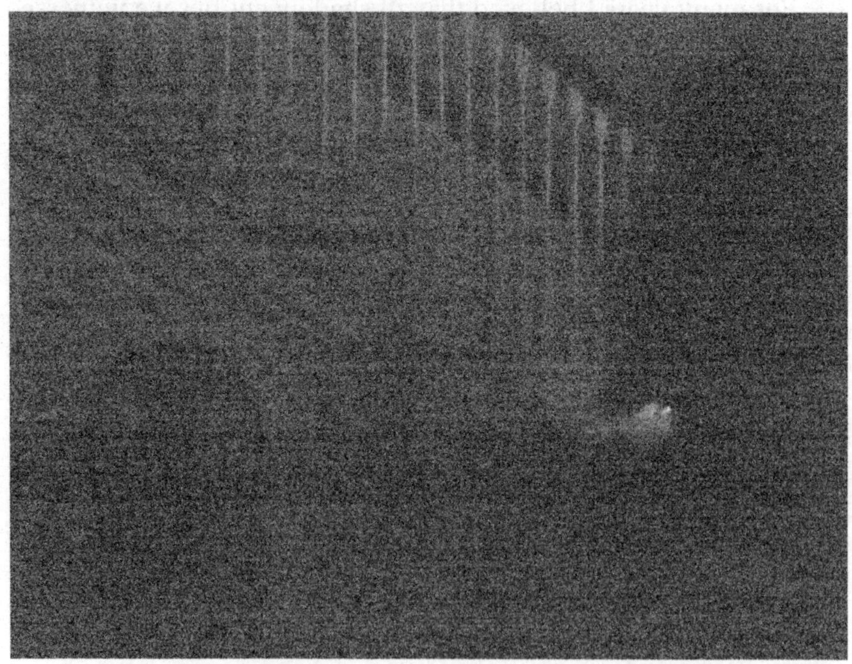

Cat Gasch's capture of a shadow entity can be seen on the right.

My friend, Cat Gasch, previously mentioned in the Hooded Figure chapter, was snapping photographs in the low-light of the candles and captured an interesting photograph of a shadow at the bottom of the stairs between a table with a candle and the railing. While the photo is grainy, it's intriguing as it makes you wonder if this may be the mysterious woman wrapped in a quilt that has been witnessed over the years.

Stairwell at Montpelier Mansion in which the woman in the quilt has been seen.

How to know the difference between interdimensional shadow beings and human spirits appearing as shadows proves to be difficult without extensive investigation and multiple experiences with the same shadow figure. Paranormal investigator Shana Wankel tells of her experiences with a little boy spirit named Byron who appeared to her as both apparition and shadow. Her first experience with Byron as an apparition is described in *Encounters With The Paranormal: Volume 2*. Below are her experiences with him as a shadow and why she believed this particular shadow person happened to be him.

Shana's Story:

In a sleepy little river town called Kampsville, Illinois, there's a building sitting on what was formerly a Native American campsite called CBC River Treasures and Cafe. In the very beginning, before there was even a building there, it was just a piece of property with a big tree on it. Near this piece of property was the site of a fight between two local residents. According to local history, a young man, Byron, climbed up the tree on the property to watch the fight but fell to his death.

His spirit liked to hang out upstairs in the building, and I feel that, for him, his spot upstairs has always been the upper branches of the tree from which he fell. We had also captured audio during various EVP (electronic voice phenomena) sessions, and on one of them, in response to a psychic medium spotting a little boy upstairs, we heard a young voice say, "I'm falling."

I'm confident enough to label him as the "Byron" from days past that was attached to the property even if we didn't find proof of his existence through extensive research. Byron has always showed up on film as a shadow, but I was also able to see him in full apparition form. I can still recall his features as plain as day from his haunting big blue eyes right down to the clothes he was wearing.

Byron used to follow me home on a weekly basis. There was one night while I was sitting on my couch reading, I saw movement in the corner of the room by the door. I glanced up to see the shadow of a small child in the corner between the front door and the door to my kids' room. I very slowly reached for my digital audio recorder which was usually sitting next to me on an end table. Back then, I used to record inside my home since there was a lot of paranormal activity going on. I turned on my recorder and asked if it was Byron. I didn't hear anything out loud, but when I told the shadow to stay away from my kids' room and not to go in, the shadow stuck its arm out and reached towards my kids' door, as if to taunt me.

I chastised the shadow figure like I would a child for bad behavior and said that if he wasn't going to listen to me, I would make him leave. The shadow never went in the room and eventually, I made a phone call to my friend, Rita, to come over. By the time she got there, the shadow was no longer in the room, which was unfortunate.

Later, when we listened to the audio that I'd recorded, a little boy's voice could be heard interacting with me. There was laughter and an, "I'll see," in response to me telling him that he'd have to leave if he didn't listen to me.

After much deliberation and experimentation, I'm pretty confident that Byron was able to shift from full human apparition form to that of a shadow figure. He's the same height in both forms, any EVPs captured on audio when both forms were spotted had the same voice, and the mannerisms were the same.

Shana's story is compelling since her involvement with the building also includes a period of time in which she worked there before the business closed down, so a familiarity had been established that didn't include work as a paranormal investigator. When she saw Byron as an apparition as depicted in the adjoining illustration, she had simply been in the building to help the owner.

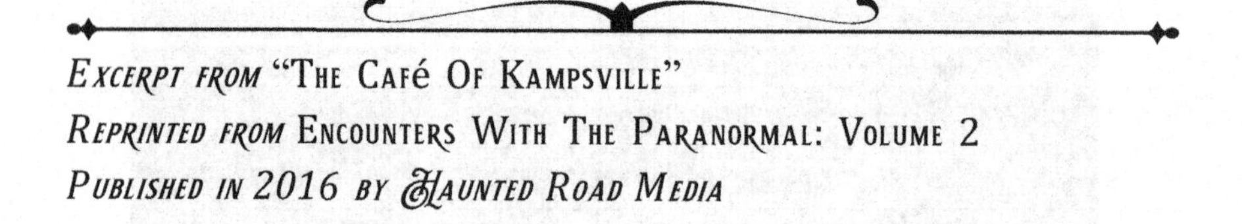

Excerpt from "The Café Of Kampsville"
Reprinted from Encounters With The Paranormal: Volume 2
Published in 2016 by Haunted Road Media

I stayed behind, alone, which is something I never did, just to see what would happen. I said, "Hello," to Byron and to anyone else inside the building who may have been listening. I announced that I didn't have any of my usual "toys" with me and that if he wanted to, he could let me see him and nobody but me would see him. I was standing in the dining room and heard a couple footsteps and a shuffling noise in the kitchen area. There was a ramp leading to it and it was on the other side of the partition separating the ramp from the kitchen where I heard the noise. I walked up the ramp and announced that I would count to three and when I said the word "three" I wanted to see him. I certainly did *not* expect for him to respect my wishes, but I gave it a shot anyway.

Right after I said, "Three," I stepped into the opening at the end of the wooden partition and looked down. For a second, I had to wonder if I was imagining what I was seeing, because standing before me was a small boy. He was about five or six years old, if I had to guess, based on his height and comparing it to my own young children. He had short, dark hair, and the biggest, widest, blue eyes that I've ever seen on a child. There was most definitely intelligence alight in those eyes, as they tracked my every movement and watched me as I was watching him. I was struck speechless that moment, and continued taking in my fill of his appearance. He was wearing a short-sleeved, white shirt and khaki or light brown shorts that were long in length. His shoes were well-worn and he was also wearing suspenders.

Prior to learning of Shana's encounters with Byron, but sometime after my evening at Montpelier Mansion, I had already been wavering in my stance that all shadows were their own type of supernatural entity. The story that seriously started changing my mind on this subject was that of Rob Gutro's aunt. I've known Rob, a gifted psychic medium, for several years, and he has developed into one of my greatest and most trusted friends. During a presentation I gave years ago for Inspired Ghost Tracking, a Maryland-based paranormal group headed up by Margaret Ehrlich, he questioned me about whether or not some shadows we witnessed could possibly be human spirits having difficulty in trying to fully manifest, then told part of the following story. Here he gives the full account in a very touching tale.

Rob's Story:

My Shadow Encounter:
My Aunt and a Story of Forgiveness
By Rob Gutro

I'm a medium and a scientist, so I use the science of energy to explain what happens to us after our physical body dies. I've learned that when there's not enough energy for an earthbound ghost or a spirit who has crossed over to show themselves in full color, they appear as shadows to the living.

I've noted in my books that we make a conscious choice after our bodies die to stay earthbound (for various reasons) and become an earthbound ghost or cross into the light and become a spirit. Ghosts usually can't move around and stay affixed to the place in which they choose to dwell, while spirits can go anywhere. My aunt seemed to be stuck between the two planes, and she connected to my energy and that enabled her to find me to beg me for help. She wanted help to totally cross over and become a spirit.

Here's the story, as it appeared in my book *Ghosts and Spirits*.

My mother's sister, Tillie, passed away in 1983.

My mother was supposed to visit Tillie the day she had a stroke. Before her scheduled visit, my Mom got the call from my aunt's neighbor who informed her my aunt was taken to the hospital. My mom raced to the hospital, located two towns away. When Mom arrived at the hospital, staff told my mother my aunt had passed.

Mom and Auntie Tillie had a sisterly love-hate relationship from what I remember. Mom told me many stories about how her sister was always causing trouble during her time among the living. She said Tillie would take some of my mother's clothes and wear them without permission.

Despite their relationship, my younger brother and I would occasionally stay with my Aunt Tillie and Uncle Richard when we were kids and we enjoyed our time together. My uncle passed in the 1970s. I loved both of them, and tried not to pay attention to the up-and-down relationship my aunt had with my mom.

A couple of weeks before my aunt passed away, my mother told me that Tillie asked for forgiveness for all of the bad things she had done to my mother during their lives. My mom said that she told her sister, "No." She refused to forgive her. I guess my mom learned about harboring grudges from her parents. Whenever I tell this story, I mention that my mother was 100% Italian, and joke that Italians invented the word "vendetta."

What's tragic is that my aunt passed away without being forgiven by my mother. I learned that's what kept her coming around. She needed forgiveness to achieve peace in the afterlife.

It's unusual for a ghost to leave a fixed location, but my aunt had been stuck here on Earth as a ghost since 1983, and over the course of 13 Earth years, she apparently learned how to move around. That's when I received her plea for help, and it was 1,090 miles from where she passed away. I later figured that she had been trying to come through to my mother and get her forgiveness, but my mom didn't recognize the signs. I believe my aunt was lingering around my mom for all that time until she connected to me.

When I moved to Kentucky in 1996, I wound up living in a haunted house. I didn't know it was haunted until after I moved into it. You can read about this startling experience in my book *Lessons Learned from Talking to the Dead*. Because the house had a resident ghost, it had negative energy in it, and sometimes that can be a magnet for other negative energy. Of course, my aunt still and always will have an energy connection with family members, including me, so she was able to "find" me over 1,000 miles from where she lived and died. Ghosts and spirits also know who is sensitive to them and can hear and see them, so that's another reason why she came to me.

One night in the Kentucky house, I was sleeping soundly when I awoke suddenly. At the foot of my bed appeared a dark shadow in the shape of a person, just standing there. It said nothing and didn't move. I immediately knew it was my aunt. When you're a medium, you can sense whether energy is good or bad. I could sense that the figure didn't want to harm me, and just wanted help.

Because it took so much energy to find me, she could only appear as a dark shadow. If she had been able to tap more energy, she could have appeared to me full-color. Because ghosts and spirits are beings of energy, they need to draw energy to strengthen and manifest. Think of how paranormal investigators go into a haunted place and ghosts in the residence drain batteries in their equipment, and then the investigators feel or hear something from the entity.

My aunt explained (telepathically) to me that she needed forgiveness from my mother so she could move into the light. The next day, I called my mother and told her what happened. She said she wanted my aunt's ghost to leave me alone. I told her that it doesn't work that way. If an earthbound ghost reveals that he or she is seeking forgiveness, they won't go away until they get it. They're bound to roam the Earth.

I explained to my mother that because my aunt Tillie's ghost was able to communicate with me once, she would be able to do it again and again until she achieves forgiveness and passes into the light. My mother said, "Tell her to leave you alone." I knew that wasn't about to happen. If a ghost has been needing something for 13 years to move on, they're not going anywhere until they get it. Just like living people.

It took 12 more years of getting requests from my aunt to get her the peace for which she begged.

From 1996 to 2008, every now and then I would ask my mother to forgive my aunt, and I would still get the "no" answer. My mom would say, "If you only knew what she did to me."

In 2008, shortly after my dad passed, I brought up the subject of my aunt's ghost again to my mother. She finally said, "I forgive her if it will help her." This time, I knew that my mother actually meant it. Since then, I haven't felt my aunt's presence. I hope she finally crossed over into the light and into the peace she's longed for.

It only took me 25 years to get my aunt the help and forgiveness she needed to achieve that final peace. In my second book, I wrote about an audible confirmation that my aunt gave me to prove she had crossed over.

*****

Entities who feel guilt over things they've done in their life on Earth may feel they don't deserve to go into the light, so they stay behind trying to get that forgiveness. Unless they can communicate with someone who knows what they need, they can remain trapped as earthbound ghosts. Being a ghost is like being trapped in an isolation jail cell for eternity and seeing those who passed into the light but they cannot communicate with them.

The lesson here is that grudges need to be released. It is critical that everyone forgive people before, or even after they pass, and really mean their forgiveness. Just saying you forgive someone doesn't work, you have to really mean it, and sometimes that really takes a lot of thought and struggle.

It's important to drop grudges and forgive people when they are alive. However, if you find you can't do that, know that you should do it after the person passes. The deceased need forgiveness to move on. It also does a living person no good to maintain grudges, especially after someone has passed away. It just allows the living person to maintain a negative energy.

Rob's story of his aunt and Shana's encounters with Byron certainly opened my mind much wider to the possibility that some shadow entities we encounter could certainly be human spirits, and I kept my mind open to that idea for several years. However, I still wasn't wholly convinced on the matter until I finally saw the phenomenon for myself during a paranormal investigation of the Mineral Springs Hotel in Alton, Illinois, following the 2019 Haunted Road Media ParaCon.

While upstairs in the top floor abandoned hotel rooms, specifically in the room known as "Pearl's Room," we heard a noise from out in the hallway and ventured out to have a look. That's when I saw her … but not at first.

She morphed out of the darkness like a rain cloud swelling in the sky. Stewing as some sort of black fog at the end of the hallway, soupy smoke billowed forth and plumed against the right wall. It surged forward, cascading against the wall then ebbing back down toward the left side of the hall only to undulate again back up the right. The shadow rocked this way like a sort of lopsided pendulum for a few moments, its density growing darker as it crept forth, yet from within that darkness a light stretched out. The dark cloud relented and it settled into a form that, at first, I almost didn't believe, but there she was, a little girl, probably around nine years old, standing in the hallway wearing some sort of dress or gown. She was a translucent white and her body faded away to nothingness near the bottom of the gown, an apparition.

"Do you see what I see?" Shana, who was present that night, had stepped next to me, also staring down the hall, but I didn't state to her what it was I saw. I wanted to hear her uninfluenced

response.

"I see her," she said. "A little girl."

One of the frequently told ghost stories of the top floor of Mineral Springs is that there's a little girl inhabiting one of the rooms off the main hallway. Visitors and paranormal investigators have left toys for her to play with, including a stuffed bear, and much time has been spent trying to deduce who she really may be. The apparition of the girl we spotted was slowly inching her way down the hall toward that room.

We spent the next several minutes trying to coax her forward, and she did cautiously start to approach us, but the girl eventually halted, stopping just short of the room in question. Eventually, we had to leave her be, and she disappeared. Whether or not she is truly the girl others have experienced in that room is unknown, but it's certainly a distinct possibility.

Rob Gutro had also once visited Mineral Springs and reported an account of the little girl in his submission to *Encounters With The Paranormal: Volume 4*: "There's another younger female presence in another of the rooms not far from Pearl's room. I feel that she looks out the window often and gazes out at the city. I often wonder if she sees the same view that we do or if she sees the city how it used to be in times past. I sometimes feel her following us when we are in the hallway going from room to room."

The illustration artist Adam D. Tillery drew for that story is also included here.

What helps my confidence with my experience that night watching the shadow morph into an apparition in the upstairs hallway is the fact that I wasn't the only one who saw the girl. Shana was with me and others who were with us saw her as well: Tom McNicholas, Dustin Sommerio, and Nick Mulae. Dustin was particularly excited since it was the first apparition he had ever witnessed. I was pretty excited, too, since I don't usually see apparitions; I mostly see shadows. Other people are just the opposite in which they may see more apparitions than shadows, and we'll talk about theories as to why that may be in Chapter 17.

Yet, here in this moment with the girl we had both shadow and apparition mixed into the same experience – from out of the darkness, light. It was a crystal-clear example that some shadow entities are truly human spirits, and I'm now forever convinced – although I still retain the right to change my mind.

The question now remains how can we tell when a shadow person is a human spirit and when it's … something else? I don't believe we're always going to know with 100% certainty, so we're going to have to put on our detective hats and execute a fair share of deduction work. The little girl transforming from shadow to apparition is obvious, but the humanoid figure standing at the end of the bed will likely be more challenging. Rob's skill as a psychic medium helped him in his case with his aunt, but not everyone is a psychic medium. For Shana with Byron, it took the captured EVPs and some reasoning from their observations to deduce that the shadow they had seen was the little boy. Even then, they cannot be absolutely sure since the shadow itself did not say, "I'm Byron, the little boy you had seen," but it most likely was.

Context is an important key to keep in mind. In Chapter 5 on hooded figures, the story of Cat Gasch's experience at the Sixteenth Century friary in Ireland was recounted in which she was saved from falling by what seemed to be some sort of figure with a hood. Considering the garb that monks and friars wore at the time the building would have been in operation, it's quite likely that this entity was the spirit of one of those monks reaching out to save Cat from a serious accident. We can never say for certain who or what grabbed her arm that day, but the history of the location does give us some insight into what it may have been.

Going back to the story with Talasyn at the house in Edmond, Oklahoma, that was featured on *The Haunted*, we did not immediately deduce that the red-eyed shadow person she had been seeing was a supernatural entity that demonologist Carl Johnson ultimately deemed a wraith. We investigated that house at least a half dozen times before Carl was brought in and performed countless hours of research outside the home to get the complete picture of what happened there. There was a distinct possibility that what Talasyn had been experiencing was the oppressive spirit of someone who had died in the home. Through hours of questioning during our EVP sessions we were able to eliminate that possibility and a clearer picture took shape over time from all the data we had been gathering. Something inhuman was at hand.

Answers to these questions are rarely given to us when we first start asking. It's from dedicated investigative work that we start fitting the pieces of the puzzle together.

Chapter 14

Shadows In The Wild

The woods and forests of the world have been regarded as mysterious and foreboding for millennia, taking on a life of their own. From the fictitious creepy woods of *Hansel and Gretel* and *Little Red Riding Hood*, even the haunted forests of *Lord Of The Rings* like Mirkwood, the Old Forest, and Fangorn, to the legends of real life sinister locations like the Hoia-Baciu Forest in Romania and its supernatural anomalies, and the dark heaviness of Japan's Aokigahara, also known as the Suicide Forest, humanity has always acknowledged a sense of dread about the vast wooded areas of the world while simultaneously being drawn to its enigmatic mystique. Countless legends and stories have been born in the wild, such as fairies, pukwudgies, sasquatch, and modern pop culture has given us thrills on the movie screen with films like the forest-dwelling *Blair Witch*, while the internet expanded a universe with its Slender Man finding a home in Nicolet Forest. Outside our comfortable homes, the untamed areas beyond are teeming with many entities we still don't understand, including shadow people.

Brittney Crabb has been recounting her paranormal experiences and sharing in her investigative adventures for over a decade on her brittyy44 YouTube channel (which can be found at http://www.youtube.com/brittyy44), as well as narrating ghost stories from around the world in very stylish fashion. Yet, through all the years, stories, and experiences, there is a shadow person encounter that remains one of her most memorable.

Brittney's Story

I was somewhere between seven to nine years old, and I was out in the forest playing with my friend, Rachel. I don't exactly remember why we felt this way, but we felt as if we were being watched by someone or some*thing*. All of a sudden, this big dark figure came out of nowhere! It was like a shadow figure and it was coming towards us!

I remember yelling, "RACHEL, RUN!" And we ran sooooo fast down that hill and back to Rachel's house scared out of our minds!

What did we see? We have no idea and even today I have no idea what that was. It definitely wasn't human. It was one of the scariest encounters I've ever had!

I've seen Brittney recount this tale more than once on her YouTube channel, and it's very apparent the encounter had significant early influence on her and her curiosity about the paranormal. Was it just a chance encounter, or was there something more ominous in those woods? She hasn't encountered this particular shadow figure in the woods since then, so there's no way to know, but it's random encounters like this that make the woods such a wild card and a premium location to experience something unusual.

When I get interviewed for radio shows and podcasts, I'm frequently asked what's been my most frightening experience, but it's really difficult to answer. People assume that since I've been on so many paranormal investigations there *have* to be a few in there that really unnerved me; however, that couldn't be further from the truth. I don't conduct investigations for jump scare thrills. For the most part, I'm simply trying to have a conversation with the spirits that may be there, these humans that no longer have a physical body. I'm in research mode, so anything that may happen that's out of the ordinary piques my interest and curiosity. I just simply don't get scared. Sorry.

That said, naturally, the shadow person I experienced in my bedroom, the one that actually touched me when I was eight or nine years old, did actually scare the shit out of me at the time. But of course, it did — I was just a little kid! The hosts of the radio shows and podcasts really want to know what paranormal activity has frightened me as an adult, and there have been zero paranormal investigations in which I was frightened by the supernatural. I've been more scared of the physical — dangerous locations and surroundings, bad neighborhoods, etc. — than anything otherworldly at the places I've investigated. However, there was one time when I *wasn't* investigating as an adult in which something surprised me that was very out of place for the situation I was in, something that completely creeped me out and made me say, "We should get out of here."

In late 2015, I made an emergency trip to Salisbury, Maryland, to talk someone off a ledge. This particular person was emotionally erratic and had returned to her childhood home which stood dark and desolate, abandoned for years before a forest of tall and ancient trees. I discovered her sitting in her parked car behind the house, and I left my vehicle in the driveway to go talk to her. The first thing I noticed as I approached her car was how much darker it was behind the house than on the side where I'd parked. I paid it no mind, however. The trees loomed large, after all, the house certainly blocked most light from the street side, and I was there for something completely personal.

I rapped on the window and she let me in the passenger side. We talked for a good long while, calming her down as the conversation prolonged, yet there was something else that just wasn't quite right. I peered into the passenger side mirror and noticed movement in the trees behind us. We continued to talk, but the movement had my attention, and I could start to see better what was back there. A group of short shadow entities were beginning to crowd around the trees, some peering out from behind the trunks while others stood directly between. This was concerning, but they were just lingering back there and there was a fair amount of distance between the house and the tree line, so I wasn't yet alarmed. That alarm sounded moments later.

My eyes continued to flit to the mirror as the conversation progressed, and the number of short shadow people continued to grow and spread amongst the trees. Every tree in the backyard now had something creeping around it, and a dark energy could be felt growing around the car. I stopped the conversation when I noticed one of the shadow entities creep out of the woods and up to the back of the car. Through the reflection I eyed it sliding in behind the car and then disappear from my view.

"I don't mean to cut you off, but we really ought to take the conversation elsewhere."

She also knew something was going on. "I feel it. It's gotten a lot darker. What did you see?"

I explained what I'd been spying in the woods and how the shadow crept up to the car. I wasn't sure if it was still waiting back there, was inching along the side, or was entering into the back seat of the car. Wherever the shadow may have been, the darkness deepened and the light around us seemed to get consumed by the night while a great weight drew down upon us.

She looked back and saw the shadows, too, but the problem was that my car was parked in the driveway and I would have to exit the vehicle to return to it. This is that one moment as an adult in which I grew nervous about a paranormal situation. I just simply wasn't prepared for this moment. I was in that creepy backyard for something completely different, and my frame of mind had been elsewhere. It's not that I thought I was going to get eaten or something ridiculous if I left the vehicle, but I wasn't sure what to expect either.

I eased out the passenger side door and slipped around the back of the car to check if the shadow had remained there. It wasn't behind the car, so I wasn't sure where it may have made off to. I glanced back into the woods at the throng of shadows that continued to gather there while a palpable electricity hovered in the air. They didn't approach, but I also didn't want to stick around to see if they would – at least not this time. At any other time in my investigative career, I would have. Then the most unexpected thing happened.

The shadows at the base of the trees had my attention, but something else was going on above them. I craned my head toward the treetops and spotted something white slinking through the branches. It was long, spindly, and amorphous sliding from one tree to another like some sort of living spider web. It made no sound as it creeped along, a silent sentinel slithering about to devour its next prey – whatever that may have been. I wasn't going to stick around and find out.

My eyes remained fixed on the tree line as I meandered backward toward my car. I wasn't going to turn my back to these strange forest entities, not with how eerily they were all moving about within the darkness. I finally slipped into the driver's seat of my car and backed it out of the driveway, the shadows still peering out from the trees the last I saw. I don't think I fully exhaled until we met at a nearby gas station and convenience store five minutes

later.

I couldn't possibly say what either of these types of entities could have been, the shadow beings around the bases of the trees or the white amorphous entity slinking its way through the tree tops. They may or may not have been related to each other, but from my quick observation I couldn't tell if they were even aware the other was there. When I think back to that particular night, I often think about how unusually dark it had been in that backyard, both in the amount of light and an overall feeling of the surroundings. It makes me wonder if there was such a lack of light of all kinds that the situation allowed for a glimpse into the world we don't usually see with our own eyes. Had the proverbial veil been pulled back for a moment in that darkness so we could see what really lurks out in the woods?

While forests are certainly a prime location for shadows to dwell, they're not limited to large groupings of trees and can also be observed elsewhere in the great outdoors. One young woman, Sierra, describes what she saw driving through the flat plains of western Illinois.

Sierra's Story

I don't know where to begin on the shadow I saw. My girlfriend, Kat, and I were driving into Kane, Illinois. I don't even remember who was driving, but right as we were nearing the Kane Cemetery, a shadow taller than a street sign walked inhumanly fast across the road into the cemetery. It was very thin and dark. It was the shape of a person but was not human. It was obviously made out of a black mass like shadows. Only I saw it. It almost completely blended in with the darkness, but thanks to the headlights, I was able to see it. The figure was darker than the darkness, but like I said, if it hadn't been for the headlights it would have blended in.

Other locations notorious for shadow entities are swamps like the Hockomock Swamp in southeastern Massachusetts in an area known as the Bridgewater Triangle. Throughout this triangle area which spans a stretch of land, water, and marsh near Abington, Rehoboth, and Freetown, people have experienced strange creatures, unexplainable lights, extraterrestrials, and other paranormal and supernatural activity. Unusual shadows are reported here, too, and many researchers believe this area may be much like the Bermuda Triangle, a vortex and gravitational anomaly, possibly even a portal to other dimensions.

Shadow people have been witnessed in most any environment, from rain forests to the frozen tundra to rugged mountains, there's really no place they don't go. That at least tells us these entities are deeply connected to this world, which may or may not be a comforting thought. If they've existed far longer than humans and have been visiting this world physically or interdimensionally for millions of years, they may actually feel that humans have been intruding on their lands, or at least lands they've been accustomed to visiting for a long time. I could tumble deep down the rabbit hole with this concept and take it all the way back to pre-history and even extraterrestrials – who is the real alien here? – but for this book I'm just going to introduce the idea that these shadow entities may have a deeper sense of ownership about our world than we currently understand.

There are several legends, both urban and cultural, that are generally reported outdoors that I am asked about routinely if they may actually be shadow people: the internet myth known as Slender Man, Skinwalkers, and Wendigos. They each carry a handful of similarities to shadow people but are not shadow people themselves. Let's take a look at each to clear up the confusion.

Slender Man and Tulpas

Slender Man was created online in 2009 as part of a Photoshop contest thread in the *Something Awful* forums by Eric Knudsen under the user named Victor Surge. The contest invited users to "create paranormal images through Photoshop" and Surge posted two photos of a tall, shadowy figure haunting children at play. He gave the photos a small story, and included with his submission a block of text that read:

"We didn't want to go, we didn't want to kill them, but its persistent silence and outstretched arms horrified and comforted us at the same time…1983 photographer unknown, presumed dead."

With a strong, positive reaction to the photos, Surge continued to post new altered photographs and added to the story of what was now being called "Slender Man," but now others on the forum began to submit their own photos and story elements as well. Dwelling deep in the forest, Slender Man is described as very tall, ranging 6 – 14 feet in height, and thin with a completely featureless white face, long arms, and tendrils or tentacles from his back which he uses to catch his prey. He wears a dark suit and tie and generally targets children. He's also supposed to have abilities in which he can read minds and teleport from one location to another.

The myth and lore of Slender Man grew, his story encompassing hundreds of pages, and an internet urban legend was born. Slender Man inspired the popular *Marble Hornets* web series, a number of independent video games, found itself a prominent position on the popular *Creepypasta* horror web site, and became the subject of countless pieces of fan art.

From the projected obscurity, a facelessness that breeds mystique, and with a storytelling vehicle that eliminates the fourth wall, Slender Man became the internet's boogeyman. The fate of his victims was also rather ambiguous and vague, fueling that mystique.

In an ironic twist, however, this boogeyman more than lures children away and does them harm. Through the created lore, Slender Man was given a background in which he was bullied, something scores of children can relate to. So, many of the children are willing to befriend the boogeyman and venture deep

Slender Man sidewalk drawing in Raleigh, North Carolina in 2012.
(Photo by mdl70, Wikimedia Commons)

into the forest with him, much like a modern-day Pied Piper.

The Slender Man myth seems to feed into what little we know about the mysterious shadow people that people have seen in real life. Tall, dark, and devoid of features, many of these mysterious entities seem to feed on fear while others simply seem curious, just standing and staring at you in the creepiest way possible. Although eerily similar, shadow people do not whisk their victims away to the forest, nor do they keep human proxies at a mansion in the forest as does Slender Man in some of his stories.

Some people believe that there may be a Slender Man *tulpa*. A tulpa is a type of supernatural entity that takes on the form of a character from legend and folklore and acts out that persona. It literally means *manifestation*. This concept originated in Tibet within early Buddhist texts about the ability to create a "mind-made body" and is the basis of the "thought form." Some beliefs include human beings creating their own tulpas purely from thought, manipulating invisible energy into visible forms. So, the idea exists that someone may have created their own Slender Man thought tulpa.

Even if this concept were to be real and some sort of entity decided to take on the persona of Slender Man, this still would not be a "real" Slender Man as described in the internet folklore. The abilities of this tulpa would be restricted to the abilities of the entity creating the tulpa. So, if it existed it would only be a mere shadow – excuse the pun – of Slender Man.

Consider another perspective on tulpas. In his book *The Mothman Prophesies*, John Keel proposes the concept of a tulpa in the very first chapter that actually has nothing to do with the famed Mothman creature and legend but the case of a haunting in New York's Greenwich Village. In an old house that has been investigated by many over the years, including Dr. Hans Holzer, a phantom in a long, black cape with a wide-brimmed hat has been seen moving about from room to room. Some say this dark, ghostly figure was a spy from the American Revolution who was caught and killed in the house.

However, this house was lived in by Walter B. Gibson, the writer who, under the pen name Maxwell Grant, created *The Shadow* pulp novels, the 1930s character who lurked in dark alleys wearing a cape and wide-brimmed hat. Prior to Gibson living in the house there had been no known reported hauntings. However, within 20 years after Gibson left his Greenwich dwelling it was suddenly haunted by the hat-wearing shadow ghost.

Keel suggested that Gibson's powerful mind constantly creating *The Shadow* stories and projecting the character out to the universe as a thought form, even unknowingly, could have created a tulpa which then became the shadow entity haunting the house in Greenwich Village. This postulates the idea that some hauntings may not be ghosts or human spirits at all – not even visitations from interdimensional beings – but something generated from the powerful human mind.

Skinwalkers

First and foremost, skinwalkers are an ancient Navajo legend, but the Navajo custom is to not discuss skinwalkers publicly for fear of retribution, so what we know about these types of entities we have to take with a grain of salt. Are we sure we have the Navajo legend correct if the Navajo aren't freely willing to discuss it?

Skinwalkers are shapeshifting entities that live in and amongst the tribe, originally a medicine man or shaman who has chosen an evil path and takes the form of an animal to inflict suffering on others. In order to become a skinwalker, the shaman must be initiated by a secret society of other skinwalkers and is required to kill a close family member. They wear the skins of the animals they transform into which is why the Navajo insist the tribe not wear the pelt of any predatory animal.

Skinwalkers are laden with many special attributes, including mind reading, controlling thoughts, the ability to jump high cliffs, and they are supposed to be able to outrun cars. They are said to be able to control night creatures such as wolves and owls to do their bidding and can also reanimate the dead to attack their enemies. Some people believe encounters with skinwalkers will generate curses, and those who cross their paths will suddenly suffer from bad luck, nightmares, and health problems. In these cases, cleansings from *good* Native American shamans are sought out to perform rituals and use sacred smoke to ward off the bad energy given to the victim by the skinwalker.

Numerous cultures from around the world have described legends of shapeshifting entities for millennia. The Greek gods were able to shapeshift. The djinn from Arabic legends are tricksters and shapeshifters. This also includes Loki in Norse traditions, Celtic fairy lore, and, of course, there are vampire legends of shapeshifting. Entities like skinwalkers may go back even further. 13,000 years ago, in a cavern in France known as "The Sanctuary," is a cave painting that's been named "The Sorcerer." It seems to have body parts of multiple animals while also having human-like arms and legs. The Sanctuary's artwork seems to depict magical ceremonies and shamanic work, so could the depiction of "The Sorcerer" be of an ancient skinwalker?

If skinwalkers are real and have any similarity to shadow entities, they may be most closely related to the crawler-type shadow person since the Navajo term "yee naaldooshii" means "with it, he goes on all fours." This is probably the biggest reason why some people ask me if skinwalkers may be a type of shadow person, but there are some other related traits as well. This entity's ability to read minds and control thoughts seems somewhat related to the hat man type shadow person who uses a telepathic means to instill fear into a victim and then feeds off that fear.

Yet, given these few related traits, I would still say skinwalkers are their own type of entity. While they may have a few sinister qualities that some shadow people also possess, there are still enough dissimilar attributes, including their origins, to put them in a supernatural category all their own.

WENDIGO

Ever since the first edition of this book, which included the section on skinwalkers, I've had more and more people question me about whether another Native American entity – the wendigo – might be a type of shadow person. Like the skinwalker, but for different reasons, the wendigo is not a form of shadow entity, but it's still rather creepy, interesting, and tragic folklore.

There are a number of variations to the wendigo story, but these creatures are mostly sighted in the forests of the Great Lakes region, Minnesota, and up into the central regions of Canada. These humanoid creatures feed on humans in order to survive the harsh winters of the area and may have begun as humans themselves, actually making them cannibals.

Basil Johnston, an Ojibwe teacher and scholar in Ontario, Canada, describes the wendigo quite vividly:

"The Wendigo was gaunt to the point of emaciation, its desiccated skin pulled tautly over its bones. With its bones pushing out against its skin, its complexion the ash gray of death, and its eyes pushed back deep into their sockets, the Wendigo looked like a gaunt skeleton recently disinterred from the grave. What lips it had were tattered and bloody. Its body was unclean and suffering from suppurations of the flesh, giving off a strange and eerie odor of decay and decomposition, of death and corruption."

The word "wendigo" can be roughly translated to mean "evil spirit that devours mankind," and devour it does. The appetite of the wendigo is said to be insatiable and never-ending, constantly feasting no matter how much it eats.

The stories are a mixture, ranging from accounts of monsters with some characteristics of a human or as an evil spirit who has taken possession of a human. Whichever the case, many of these have grown to a height of about 15 feet and possess glowing eyes, sharp claws, and yellowed fangs licked over by an extra-long tongue. While these creatures are gluttonous and constantly eating, they appear as if they're on the brink of starvation.

Yet, other legends state the wendigo are agile, possess a great deal of speed, and have outstanding stamina to survive the long winters. These legends also state the wendigo can mimic human voices and lure people out into the forests toward them. Once the person is isolated, the wendigo attacks and devours the human.

Robert Fiddler, son of Jack, who succeeded his father as chief of the Sucker peoples and Deer Lake Band.

According to some Algonquian legends, a wendigo spirit is created whenever a human resorts to cannibalism, an unfortunate tragedy that was known to occur amongst tribes as people grew hungry during dark, bitter winters. In the early 1900s, there was an Oji-Cree chief named Jack Fiddler who was also a medicine man and known far and wide for his powers to conjure animals and to defeat wendigos. Fourteen wendigos are said to have fallen by Jack's hand, many of which were said to have been sent by enemy shamans. Still yet, others were known to be cannibals and craved to eat human flesh. In these cases, Jack was usually asked by a family to kill a sick member before they "turned wendigo," and one of these cases included Jack's brother Peter Flett. Peter was on a trading expedition that ran out of food and he, ultimately, resorted to cannibalism. Several cases like this were recorded in the records of the Hudson's Bay Company Traders.

Eventually in 1907, Jack Fiddler and his brother, Joseph, were tried for the murder of Joseph's daughter-in-law in a wendigo case, and the two men plead guilty. Jack stated the girl was on the verge of transforming into a wendigo and needed to be killed before she murdered and ate other members of the tribe.

Swift Runner incarcerated after "turning wendigo" and cannibalizing his family.

These are sad stories. Predating Jack and Joseph was Swift Runner, a Native American who, in 1879, murdered and ate his entire family that winter, claiming he was possessed by the wendigo spirit.

Perhaps, it's the overall supernatural element to some of these legends and stories that have caused people to question whether the wendigo is actually some kind of shadow entity, but that really doesn't appear to be the case. Modern anthropologists believe the wendigo legends only developed after Native Americans came into contact with European settlers and resources started to grow scarce. With food supplies suddenly lower than normal, these tribes may have developed a fear of starvation to fuel the stories of the evil spirits that devour mankind. However, if the legends *do* predate European settlement the stories still lack any similarity to that of shadow beings. If anything, the wendigo folklore most resembles that of our modern-day flesh-eating zombie stories, a far cry from shadow people, and those confirmed cases in which people murdered and resorted to cannibalism during harsh, bleak winters are truly horrible.

Chapter 15

The WTF Shadows

With the number of people that have reached out to me over the years about shadow people, there are several accounts which I would file away in what we sometimes call the "WTF File." There are bizarre reports that are seemingly related but they don't really fit into any of the categories we have established. We humans truly like to categorize things, but perhaps, since our degree of understanding of these entities is so limited, we simply just don't have a very good means in which to organize.

One bizarre report came from a woman who approached my table after I spoke at a conference, and she proceeded to tell me about a rather unusual short shadow person with both a pointy head and a pointy chin. The way she described it I couldn't help but imagine this entity being a dwarf or maybe even a large gnome with a crescent moon-shaped head.

Dark in the house, walking toward the bathroom, she turned and saw it dart into her son's room. She immediately dashed into his room, but the odd creature wasn't there. After this event, she consulted an intuitive to see if she should be concerned about this shadow entity that had entered her son's room, and the intuitive gave a reading that included her son shooting somebody.

The woman's son later injured a girl in the neck with a paintball gun. Whether that had anything to do with this oddly-shaped shadow person is completely unknown.

The aforementioned Black Bear Church in Olive Township, Oklahoma, has much more than just the crawler-type shadow entity creeping around the premises. The local legend of Black Bear Church is that sometime after the parish had closed its doors and the building fell derelict and in disrepair, an occult group began to frequent the property late at night to conduct an assortment of rituals. According to the story, during one of these rituals they managed to conjure the dark entity which we've come to know as the crawler, and it claimed the building for its own, making it its domicile on Earth.

Along with this dark entity are said to have come forth smaller shadow minions, short and stocky in nature. According to local paranormal investigative teams, this group of strange, small shadow people do not actually enter the building but remain outside and peer in through the windows. They're creepy, and there's plenty of speculation as to their function, whether that's as guardians to the crawler or even as worshippers of this dark entity. These short shadow minions are also known to grope and scratch at cars parked on the property and have been witnessed at times clawing at cars driving away from the church at night. Some have reported actual handprints or claw marks appearing on their vehicles after driving away.

In March 2018, I conducted a paranormal investigation of the Madison Seminary in Madison, Ohio, piggy-backing off an investigation with the then-Ohio Paranormal Syndicate. The seminary was established in 1847 to provide higher education for men and women of Lake County and beyond. It grew and served in this capacity until 1891 when it was purchased by the Ohio Women's Relief Corps and was designated the "Ohio Cottage" which added Army nurses from the Civil War, as well as wives, sisters, and mothers of the soldiers who fought. Since 1962, when the Women's Relief Corps ceased operations it has been many things, but now it is a destination for paranormal investigators to research supernatural activity.

Madison Seminary, Madison, Ohio. The building with the columns in the rear of the photo is the original building where I was cursed at on the top floor.

There's a story about the original seminary building that on the top floor there is a periodic shadow entity that has been seen there, but it is quite unlike many other shadow people. This one takes the form of a gorilla, or at least, it seems gorilla-like in its shape. Although I didn't actually witness this gorilla shadow entity while I was conducting my own personal investigation away from the rest of the group, I heard quite a bit of shuffling and moving around throughout that floor of the seminary. Most poignant of all, however, was the EVP (electronic voice phenomenon) I captured that cursed me out when I walked through the doorway in which the gorilla-shaped entity is seen. There's no way to know if this capture was the gorilla shadow entity voicing its displeasure, unseen but still present.

Sometimes we have a WTF moment with shadow entities when the activity concerns, not only the shadow entity itself, but other entities as well. Aboard the now-lost *Goldenrod Showboat*, we frequently saw a shadow entity and experienced heavy energy in a short passage that connected the upper-level dining room with the balcony of the *Goldenrod*'s showroom. However, there was one particular evening during an investigation in which paranormal investigator Shana Wankel observed this shadow activity with a little something extra in tow.

Shana's Story:

During a paranormal investigation on the *Goldenrod Showboat* one cold evening, I felt compelled to wander upstairs to the dining room, which had once been the former living quarters, on my own. I usually never separated myself from whomever was there with me, but on this particular night, there was something or someone drawing me upstairs.

I climbed the stairs very slowly, and as I reached the top of the stairs, I saw movement across the room. As my eyes acclimated to the darkness, what I saw was a tall shadow figure walking through the doorway into the next room. All I could see was a head, shoulders, and torso, but no legs or feet. It's a possibility that the shadow figure was wearing a dress since the shadow extended to the floor. Directly behind the shadow figure were two anomalies that we refer to as "twinkles," following single file, and evenly spaced apart. In scale to the shadow figure, I'd say the twinkles were about waist high. There was no sound to be heard and none of the entities responded to my voice.

Low-light video screen capture of the doorway off the Goldenrod*'s dining room where Shana had seen the twinkles follow the shadow. Other investigators frequently saw a shadow figure here, and anytime I walked through the passageway to the balcony beyond I felt a dark, heavy presence.*

This is the only time that I'm aware of in which someone observed what seemed like clear interaction between the shadow that lurked in that passage and the twinkles that had become more commonplace during the final year the *Goldenrod* was accessible (after a legal struggle, it was destroyed in an arson fire). Could the shadow have been leading the twinkles somewhere or were the twinkles chasing off the shadow? Unfortunately, we'll never know.

With lack of any other reference, those who witnessed the twinkles believed they may have been some sort of fairy activity.

This is a difficult line of research, firstly because of the negative stigma associated with even saying the word "fairy," and secondly, because most research on the subject leads one down a path heavily laden with legend and folklore which has been compounded over the centuries. Trying to find that nugget of original truth is difficult with these entities, so it's almost like starting back at square one. I don't believe these "twinkles" were directly associated with the shadow person in the passage since we had seen them so many other times on the showboat without the presence of the shadow, but it's interesting that they were able to see and interact with it.

Chapter 16

Shadows In The Matrix

"Aber was ist, wenn Gott keine Ahnung hat, was er tut?"
"But what if God doesn't know what he's doing?"
—Mikkel, *Dark* (Netflix Series)

In 1999, the blockbuster movie *The Matrix* introduced the masses to the concept that humanity may actually be living in a computer simulation. For those that missed this popular hit film, the Matrix is a computer-generated dream world constructed by a race of machines to keep humans, their source of electric power, subservient without realizing they're slaves. While the real world is a savage wasteland, those plugged into the Matrix are able to experience a simulated universe modeled after the late Twentieth Century, making them unaware their life experience is actually a fantasy.

There are many who believe this is not far from the truth, that we do live in a real-life version of the Matrix, perhaps not exactly as the movie depicts, but that the world around us is just a simulation. First, let's define what exactly a simulation is, and while I have a degree in Simulation Programming and could write out a basic definition, I'm going to the cite the words of Gregg

Braden, a best-selling author of consciousness literature who became the first Technical Operations Manager for Cisco Systems in 1991, and was a 2020 nominee for the prestigious Templeton Award which was established to "honor outstanding individuals who have devoted their talents to expanding our vision of human purpose and ultimate reality." In the second season of his Gaia network series *Missing Links*, Braden states in the "Evidence Of Our Simulated Reality" episode, "A simulation is an experience that allows us to immerse ourselves in an unfamiliar environment, first, and second, it allows us to master the parameters of that environment in a relatively safe way while minimizing the risk of injury to ourselves or to one another."

What strikes me about this statement is the piece on mastering the parameters of our environment. Those that believe in reincarnation often state that we come to the world to learn a lesson, and we keep returning lifetime after lifetime to learn more and more, lesson after lesson, until we ascend to some higher level of consciousness. Much of that sounds like mastering parameters to me.

While for this chapter you have to assume that the Matrix, or something like it, is real, that we are actually living in some sort of simulation whether it is computer-generated or it is some other form of technology, possibly even organic and biological, that this simulation is a false world in which we currently live and have our experience of reality, how far is that from most of the religious belief systems around the world?

Braden continues to tell us,

> "The characteristics of a simulated world – a simulation has a place where it begins, a definite beginning, and it has a place where it ends. And what happens in between that beginning and the ending is based on a mathematic algorithm, a rhythm of cycles in patterns that repeat again

and again and again on different scales.

In a simulation, there are rules that govern the simulation, and the idea is that as the people in the simulation become more familiar with the environment, as they learn those rules, life gets better. They improve with practice.

In a simulation, the users always have access to an external reality that they can tap into for guidance if they get into trouble or if they need clarification. They always have the ability to communicate beyond the simulation itself.

And in a simulation, the user cannot tell the simulation from the real world."

Having access to an external reality for guidance sounds very similar to the idea of spirit guides or praying to a higher power for guidance or help, something billions of people do every day. I briefly touched on belief systems a moment ago, each in their own context essentially describing humanity living in a simulated world. Braden breaks that down a bit further:

"The Sanskrit word *maya* actually means illusion. This is a fundamental concept in the Hindu tradition. … They tell us that it is under the illusion, under maya's influence, that the soul identifies with the body to the point where we cannot tell ourselves as separate from the illusion of this physical world. Under maya's influence, we get lost in the body's expressions of ego and fear, sex, race, the color of our skin, our belief systems under the illusion of maya. In those same traditions, the idea of enlightenment means to escape the maya, to escape the illusion.

Christian traditions tell us something very, very similar. They tell us almost universally the world is temporary, that

> it is an illusion, not to get stuck here, that we're here only briefly, and that we are preparing. They actually say we're preparing ourselves to live in another world. … This parallels the ideas of a simulation almost to a t."

On a technological note, John D. Barrow, cosmologist, theoretical physicist, and mathematician, states, "It has long been recognized that technological civilizations, only a little more advanced than ours, will have the capacity to simulate universes in which self-conscious entities can emerge and communicate with one another."

So, while this is fascinating, what does all of this have to do with shadow people? If our existence in this world is a simulation, what exactly are shadow entities within the construct of a situation such as living in the Matrix?

Consider there is a "real world" outside of our own, far beyond the boundaries of the universe. If this is true, then it is possible that the shadow people we witness of all varying types could possibly be some sort of person from this real world who has accessed the simulation and is interacting with it on their own level. Perhaps, with their type of access to the simulation they are not able to fully manifest as a human within the environment and appear as a shadowy form. What their aim is, one can only guess; however, so many shadow people are witnessed as entities that are observing human beings. Perhaps, if this is somebody from the real world entering into the simulation, they may be simply acting as an observer of the simulation and noting the interactions and tendencies of a particular person. I think back to the hat man situation with the three sisters and how he simply stood at the end of the bed of the one, staring down and just observing her. Was he taking in information about her sleep patterns and rhythms? Did he do the same for the next person who moved into that house, in that room? Was he actually assigned to that room as if it was his job, perhaps earning $15 per hour, or its equivalent, in the real world?

For some of those more nefarious type of entities, perhaps there's a higher agenda we simply don't understand, conflicting powers from the real world who have taken their battles into the simulation. If we have a consciousness in that real world with its own set of values that has taken a side in some sort of extra-universal struggle, perhaps those enemies seek us out here.

Likewise, it's possible these shadow people are almost like deadly agents from the film *The Matrix*. The role of these beings in the film were not as inherent parts of the simulation but were programs from the outside, other entities from the machine world who were sent into the simulation to perform a job and a function to hunt down other entities (the awakened humans) who did not belong within the Matrix simulated world. Or perhaps it's possible that these shadow people are like one of the rogue programs from the real machine world which is trying to seek refuge within the simulation.

When alien abductees talk about implants (some of which have really been pulled out of victims), perhaps this is an implant from the real world in order to track the human within the simulation world. Again, I harken back to *The Matrix* when the agents implant a tracking device inside Neo to keep tabs on his whereabouts within the virtual reality. There are a variety of different theories we can consider. It's almost limitless, and our imaginations can run wild, but I believe it's good practice to let our imaginations run free here and take into account all possibilities.

In Nick Bostrom's 2003 paper published in *Philosophical Quarterly*, "Are You Living In A Computer Simulation," he has a different take on shadow people in a simulated world, "In addition to ancestor-simulations, one may also consider the possibility of more selective simulations that include only a small group of humans or a single individual. The rest of humanity would then be zombies or 'shadow-people' – humans simulated only at a level sufficient for the fully simulated people not to notice anything suspicious. It is not clear how much cheaper shadow-people would be to simulate than real people. It is not even obvious that it is possible for an entity to behave indistinguishably from a real human and yet lack conscious experience."

In other words, in this scenario, in order to fill out the simulation with a populace to make it appear to the experiencer that the world is real, "shadow people" are inserted into the virtual space to help the viewer buy into the simulation. While not exactly a shadow as we've come to define shadow people throughout the rest of this book, it does harken to a type of entity that is soulless and with a purpose that is simply utilitarian. However, I find it interesting that he uses the term here. It certainly makes you wonder about some people you observe aimlessly ambling about the aisles at the grocery store. Are they really just filler?

In many ways, I like to think of this simulation scenario as a Game Master entering into a Massively Multiplayer Online Game to view what may be happening within the game space. While players generally don't realize the GM is there since the GM is usually invisible, there are occasional moments in which the Game Master may slip up and the player suddenly has an idea the GM is there. If we look at shadow people as Game Masters, or some other functioning entity from the outside world entering our "game space" here on Earth, then it stands to reason there may be periodic moments in which we can actually observe the presence of one studying us.

I have one other suggestion on the matter of simulations, a topic that really deserves its own lengthy text, and we'll likely perform a deep dive later in a different text. Most of the literature and conversation I've consumed on this topic has regarded these simulations in the environment of the electronic computers we're familiar with today. Perhaps, that's because we've seen the power of what these electronics can do today compared to the technology we had just a hundred years ago. However, I think we're limiting ourselves to the construct of modern human ingenuity and technology, and that this simulation we live within is not built upon computer hardware as we understand it today (or even tomorrow).

I believe this simulation is more biological, perhaps even molecular in nature, and that we, as humans, are a part of that so-called computer. Perhaps, that is why something on such a massive scale is so easily powered. While science is still coming to grips on the complexities of the human brain, spiritualists are still coming to grips with the vastness of how interconnected the entire universe really is.

The idea of *quantum entanglement* has become increasingly popular these days, the phenomenon in which two or more objects separated at a distance have instantaneous influence over each other. The connection of the objects is not a matter of sending a signal to one that the other has been affected, but their connection through entanglement means that when something happens to the one it simultaneously happens to the other no matter how great the distance is between the two.

I believe this is still just scratching the surface of how the universe is really connected. It certainly seems to be the right path and does start explaining how on a molecular level objects are connected to each other, but I still believe it's much deeper than we currently speculate, that there's a world around us that we don't usually see, that is veiled to our human eyes, but on occasion we get a glimpse of what that world may be.

And shadow people happen to be a part of that world we don't quite yet understand.

CHAPTER 17

INTERDIMENSIONAL SHADOWS

Dr. Hans Holzer was one of the founding fathers of the modern paranormal field and is widely credited with coining the term "Ghost Hunter" after his landmark book of the same name, published in 1963[1]. With a doctorate in philosophy, he was the first academic to really embrace the paranormal and went on to write 145 books.

His take on the supernatural, or what we have mostly been calling paranormal these days thanks to the bevy of ghost-themed television shows in circulation, is that it's not "supernatural" at all. All of this phenomenon is entirely a part of this universe; therefore, it is quite natural, indeed.

In an interview with Reverend Laurie Sue Brockway, an author, teacher, and contemporary clergy person who specializes in matters of the heart and soul, in 1999, Holzer stated, "Belief is the uncritical acceptance of something you can't prove. I work on

[1] The term "ghost hunter" was in use prior to Holzer's book in 1963. We have found it in newspaper articles dating back to the 1800s, but one could easily say that Holzer popularized it, brought it to the mainstream, and is the reason so many people call themselves ghost hunters today, including the television show of the same name.

evidence; I either know or I don't know. There are three dirty words in my vocabulary: belief, disbelief, and supernatural. They don't exist. There's no 'supernatural world.' Everything that exists is natural. Yet, there is a dimension of existence that is as real as your living room, even if the average person cannot access it with all their senses. I coined the phrase 'the other side' because it really is the other side, like one side of the mirror. The spirit world, or 'the world next door,' as Eileen Garrett[2] called it, is not up or down. It is here, moving at a different rate of speed."

I've enjoyed saying for years that there is another world around us that we don't normally see with our own eyes, but occasionally we're able to interact with it or catch glimpses of it. This parallels nicely with Holzer's idea that "the other side" is here, just moving at a different speed. In the circles I frequent, we talk at times about "vibrational level," the energy frequency that surrounds and permeates every cell in our bodies. It is different for everyone since this personal resonance is a reflection of one's thoughts, feelings, and beliefs, and I believe it allows everyone to experience and see the spirit world, the other side, in different ways. Perhaps, it is even a part of our DNA, a genetic predisposition to interface with the spiritual world in specific ways.

Freddy Silva, a best-selling author, and one of the world's leading researchers of ancient systems of knowledge, alternative history, and the interaction between temples and consciousness states in *The Divine Blueprint: Temples, Power Places And The Global Plan To Shape The Human Soul*, "The human body is an aggregate of an energy field, and that field is interconnected to everything that exists. Energy is the engine that drives everything including our own consciousness, and as such, energy can influence us and we can influence it. This energy field is a force

---

[2] Eileen Garrett was a renowned, yet controversial, Irish medium and parapsychologist in the Twentieth Century (1893 – 1970).

and it is full of information, or as Einstein succinctly stated, 'the field is the only reality.'"

While working with paranormal investigator Shana Wankel, she and I used to joke around that on an investigation I was the light to her darkness and she the darkness to my light. It was really just our differing personalities, and perhaps, the way we handled these investigations. While she was deeper into the "witchy shit" (as she liked to say), I certainly take a more academic approach to my research, even though I absolutely do have a genuine interest in all things mystical, have my own little collection of stones, and I even have a few sets of Tarot cards. Our differences at this level also extended to the type of paranormal activity we observed. Shana is the type of person who sees more apparitions and fewer shadows while I see more shadows and fewer apparitions. Could this be due to the fact that our personal vibrational frequencies are resonating at different levels? It's likely, and so as that world around us is moving at a different rate of speed as Holzer suggests, and it's all interconnected as Silva states, Shana and I were able to interact with the world and that energy during those investigations in different ways.

What's also interesting is Andrea Perron in her trilogy *House of Darkness House of Light*, her family's memoirs living a decade in what has now become known as *The Conjuring* House (after the movie which depicts the haunting of their family), describes a type of supernatural "bubble" she and her sisters would occasionally enter into in which space and time acted differently. For what seemed like twenty or thirty minutes, those who entered the bubble would experience off-the-wall paranormal activity, yet when they exited, the amount of time that had actually passed had only been about two minutes. Talk about a different rate of speed! There are many things about this universe we can't yet explain, but according to Dr. Holzer, all of these things are still quite natural.

While interviewing him for *The Shadow Dimension* docu-series, my colleague, esoteric researcher Jonny Enoch, described shadow beings he encountered that he believed were interdimensional in nature. Jonny has been researching extraterrestrial phenomena and esoteric subjects for over 20 years, and his investigations have revealed an intelligent blueprint found within our ancient religions and symbolism while exploring quantum physics, the multiverse, and ET contactee testimonials. Below is an excerpt from that interview.

JONNY ENOCH SHADOW DIMENSION ZOOM INTERVIEW

November 12, 2020

"About 13 years ago, I had a strange experience when I was coming home one Saturday afternoon. It was in the middle of the day. I walked up to the master bedroom, and I was going to get changed after being out for the better half of the day. As I went up there, I turned on the light for the master bedroom and the walk-in closet which was sort of adjacent to where the bed and everything was. The windows were open, the light was coming in, and it was broad daylight. This wasn't at night, or anything dark or spooky, or anything like that.

As I walked into the room, all of a sudden, I saw these three beings appear behind the door, and they had this strange substance to them. I could see an outline of them. They were sort of transparent, yet I knew that there was a very ominous presence to them. I could feel them. I knew they were there, and it was such a strong overpowering feeling that I could feel it into my very being. All of a sudden, I started backing up further and further away as they were approaching me; they started to come towards me. As this was happening, I found myself going up into the back of the bed. I'm pushing myself up against the duvet and everything going back up against the wall, and I'm telling them they have to leave.

I'm using anything I can say, like, 'You have to go now,' and, 'Go to the light.'

The strange thing is that this was not just like an ordinary ghost or an apparition or anything like that. These were very clearly what people have described as shadow beings. Over the years, I had heard people talk about shadow beings, and I kind of dismissed it, and I thought those are just stories people tell. But I most very clearly saw these beings.

They started to approach me; they started getting closer and closer. They came almost up to the end of the bed, and at that point I was like, *Are they going to do something to me?* Because I legitimately felt them. I was terrified in that moment. I finally said one more time again, 'Go now,' and a click took place in the master bedroom where the light shut off, like physically shut off. The light went off to the walk-in closet and into the back room that that was connected to the master bedroom.

I started yelling in the middle of the day. People came up from the lower half of the house, and they're all shaken up [and asking], 'What's going on? What's happening?'

I was white as a ghost. I had just seen and encountered the shadow beings.

I tend to think that these were interdimensional beings. I've heard people talk about ghosts and spirits, apparitions, and what their encounters are like, and I've even seen some of the ghostly figures before when I stayed in castles in Europe. I've seen things out of the corner of my eyes. These beings – I would describe the encounter was much different. There was something about them that ... it was like, "What is this? Who are they?" I tend to think they're from another dimensional space.

We know now that we live in a multiverse. In fact, we live in a multidimensional multiverse, and how we know that is through something known as the Wilkinson's Microwave Anisotropy

Probe. What it tells us is that the radioactive background of our universe has these patterns in the background, these circuitous patterns. And these patterns are indicative that our universe is replicating itself. Not only is it expanding, it's growing, and as you mentioned there is this universe that has existed before it, but there are other universes. And what we now believe in our cosmological theories, in our theoretical physics, is that we live in a vast ocean full of universes with these little bubbles, and they're all connected.

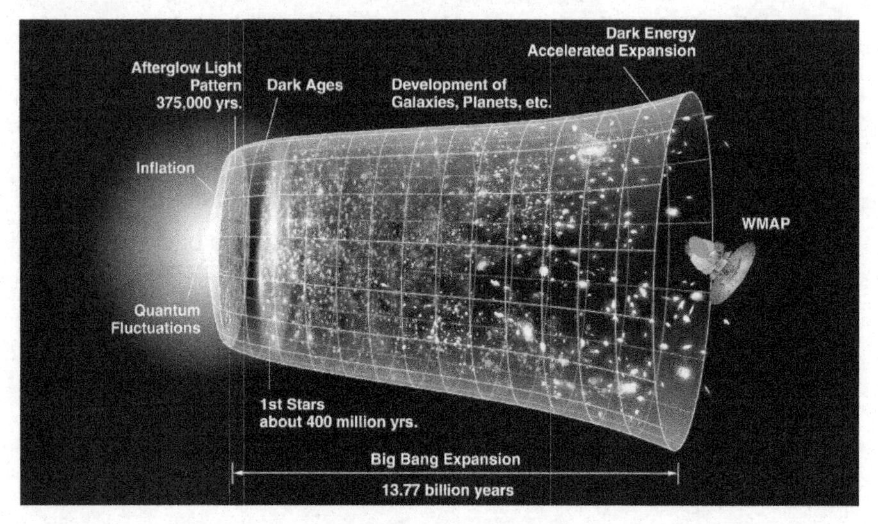

Illustration by the NASA/WMAP Science Team depicting the expansion of the universe as observed by Wilkinson Microwave Anisotropy Probe (WMAP).

The real question we have to ask ourselves is where are these shadow beings coming from? Are they in a dimensional space from *our* universe? Could they be traversing here from *other* universes?"

In my research, I like to find connections, and what I find interesting is both Andrea and Jonny used the descriptive term "bubble" to describe this type of phenomenon. While Jonny's explanation was on a much larger scale, describing the cosmos and multiple universes, as opposed to the Perron family's experiences in a Rhode Island farmhouse, the structure is essentially the same. When we think of *wormholes* in our universe, we usually envision a circular tunnel connecting one point in space with another, but a circle in three-dimensional space is actually a sphere – a bubble. Could the bubble in Andrea's former home actually be connected to one of the universes Jonny described, allowing for wormhole-like travel in between?

True Shadow People

"What are shadow people?" is a question I get all the time, and there's no real straightforward answer, nothing you can wrap up in a nice little box and put a bow on it. I've maintained that an experience with a shadow could be an experience with any number of different things. Another quote from *The Shadow Dimension* docu-series I think is very poignant came from Psychic Explorer Mark Anthony (also known as The Psychic Lawyer). In Episode 1, he states, "We may very well be dealing with several different entities, several different species using a similar energetic modality in order for them to communicate or to visit what we call Earth."

As we've seen, they take any number of different shapes and forms, they each seem to have their own agenda, for better or worse, but each of these entities come into our world utilizing some sort of shadow form, or as Mark so eloquently said, "a similar energetic modality." While this is certainly the case, and I used that quote twice during an interview I filmed for an episode of *Ancient Aliens*, at some point we have to point an arrow somewhere and say, "Ok, this is what a 'true' shadow person is," even if there are a bevy of different kinds. It's just human nature to define these sorts of things, to categorize and compartmentalize.

That said, like Jonny Enoch, I believe true shadow people are interdimensional beings. They are a part of this universe, but they generally operate on a different plane of existence than our own, a different dimension, so we don't usually see them. However, there are times in which their frequency from that plane of existence resonates at a different level than usual, something closer to ours, and we are able to catch a glimpse, perhaps even have a full interaction with them on occasion. There are times in which this seems unintentional and other times in which it seems this is the way they actually travel to our dimension in order to purposefully do some sort of action in our world.

The first shadow person interaction I had when I was eight or nine years old with the entity who crossed my arms across my body, this certainly seemed like an intentional interaction. It's still debatable as to what that intention was, but there was still some sort of purpose behind it. The same can be said for the entity with red eyes that terrorized Talasyn in Edmond, Oklahoma, the shadow that led Sandra and Keith Johnson to a cemetery behind a historic building, the crawler circling the basement room at Black Bear Church, and any number of the Old Hag accounts.

Take into consideration the shadow entity incident in Chapter 10 in which the woman related her story to me about the flashes of light and the subsequent shadow man that sat on her chest. Were those flashes of light possibly the entity entering our plane of existence and then later exiting? Was this an intentional crossing of one dimension to another that required such a transfer of energy that it created a burst of light? Was the wiring damaged in the room or did some sort of residue from that energy transfer remain in her house so that when she flipped the light switch in that room and added power to the wiring it destroyed the electronic components on that circuit?

The incident, however, that confirmed for me that true shadow people are interdimensional beings was the shadow wisp in the kitchen at Johnny V's restaurant described in Chapter 6. If you recall, I had seen the shadow wisp dart across the kitchen, I – and everyone else there – heard it bang into the flimsy swinging metal door, and yet the door didn't move at all. It remained completely stationary. Those three things together in our conventional world don't make any sense at all, but in a universe with multiple dimensions and planes of existence it's completely possible.

Here's what I think happened: Some sort of entity was in that kitchen when I walked in, and it was resonating as just a vague bit of shadow. When I walked in and it saw me, I scared *it* and it took off running through the door. On the shadow's plane of existence that flimsy metal door blew wide open as it ran away from me, yet I couldn't see that happen because the door remained stationary on *my* plane of existence. Yet sound is on a different wavelength and has its own frequency, so perhaps, that sound of the door being slammed into and its vibration resonated across both dimensions. While I couldn't see what actually happened on the shadow's plane of existence, I could certainly hear it.

These last two paragraphs are really the crux of this entire book. Please take a moment to carefully read those again and walk through the moment. What I experienced – and what that shadow person experienced – in that moment happened in multiple dimensions. It happened on two different planes of existence that were overlapping each other for a short period of time. I stood shocked for a brief moment, the shadow entity, scared, ran off, and everyone heard the crash of the metal door. A lot of things happened in the span of about three seconds, but those three seconds have made a world of difference in the way I have viewed the supernatural – or natural – world ever since.

The adjoining illustration tries to depict this scenario with the shadow person I encountered on its own plane of existence on the top half of the diagram and my world on the bottom. You have to use a bit of imagination since this is a 2D representation of something that is at least four dimensions. The line through the middle depicts a dimensional divide, although we're really encompassing the same space, and serves as that separator between the shadow's experience and my own. That divide, however, is able to be penetrated by sound in this case, and that resonance is shown emanating from the door in the shadow's dimension and into our world. Why did it penetrate that divide this time and not every time we see a shadow person? We could postulate any number of theories, but we really don't know at this point. One other theory to consider is that these aren't really different dimensions we're looking at here as they are different points in time.

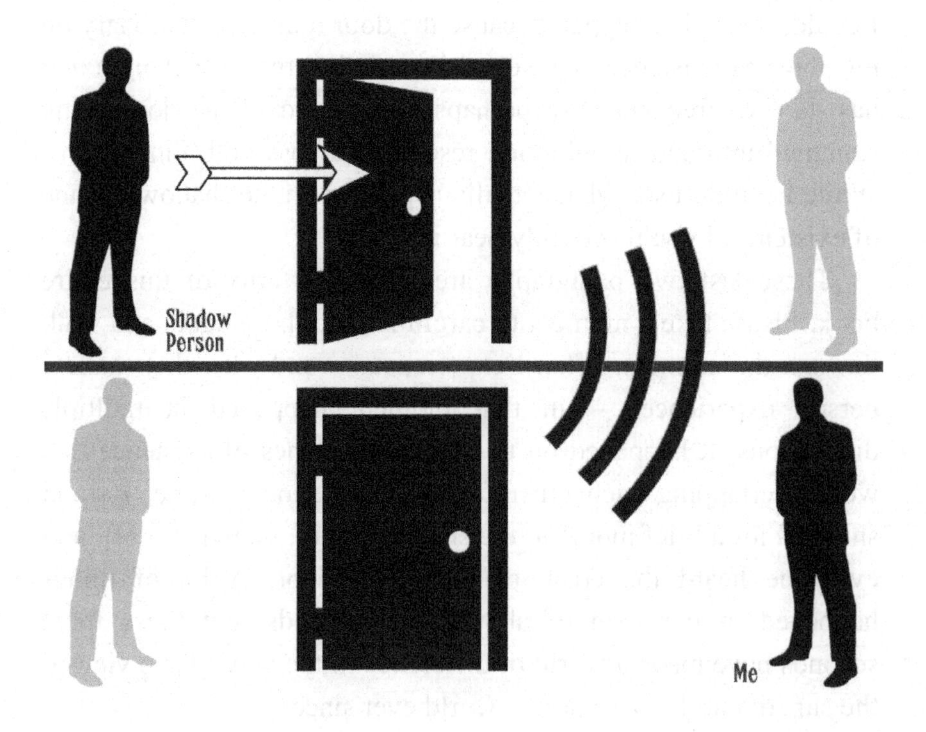

In Keith Johnson's summation of what his wife, Sandra, experienced in State College, Pennsylvania, he stated that she, "also theorizes that they can be a form of time displacement." This is interesting, because if these shadow entities are resonating on a different frequency than humans, then they may be experiencing time differently than us. I already have many theories about time which are beyond the scope of this book, including the concept that time doesn't exist, that everything is actually happening concurrently, and humanity has simply invented the concept of a "river of time" to describe the way we experience what is really the fourth dimension. If our personal resonance and vibration allows us to experience time in the particular fashion we usually do, i.e. 60 seconds in a minute, 60 minutes in an hour, 24 hours in a day, etc., then a being from another dimension resonating at a different frequency likely experiences time differently. Perhaps time is faster to these entities and that's why they're able to move about so quickly. Or maybe it moves slower, and when it seems to us they're standing in the corner being creepy for 20 minutes it's really more like 20 seconds. Perhaps time doesn't operate like a river to these beings, and it's more like an elevator in which they can simply choose a floor to access a different time period. We could come up with dozens of different theories and ideas on this alone, but the point is that if shadow people resonate differently and that's why they typically reside in another dimension, then it's likely they also experience time in a different fashion. It's probably another reason why their actions seem so peculiar to us during those brief moments when we're actually able to see them.

A variation of a time displacement would be a *time slip*, a moment when images from a past – or even future – era are observed within our own reality, including people in period clothing, structures, and wildlife with whom the observer is actually able to interact. One of the more well-known stories of this kind is the Versailles Time Slip in 1901 in which two middle-aged English women, Eleanor Jourdain and Charlotte "Annie" Moberly, were walking through the gardens of the Palace of Versailles when they noticed that the other people around them were suddenly dressed very differently and quite similar to those during the Eighteenth Century prior to the French Revolution.

These people included a pockmarked man on the step of a summerhouse, as if he'd contracted small pox, and a woman in an Eighteenth Century gown drawing a sketch of Marie Antionette. In addition to the people, they also spotted a plough in the garden although there hadn't been a plough present there since the reign of King Louis XVI.

Can shadow people be observations of time slips? Can the shadows we see possibly be images from another time and place starting to manifest in our own plane of existence but don't completely take shape? Could the shadow entity I witnessed at Johnny V's be a time slip in which I actually witnessed an image of someone who had previously worked in the building … or is going to work there in the future?

Extraterrestrials

When I give lectures about shadow people, a question I commonly receive during the Q&A portion or as side conversation afterward is, "Are shadow people aliens?" The question became so popular, I started including this topic as a part of the presentation and sometimes speak on just this interest alone.

This is actually a very good question since there are likely a large variety of different types of extraterrestrials throughout our universe, and we still have many different ideas and theories as to how they interact with us in our own world. Most people want to see little green men in round flying saucers appear on their doorstep and say, "Hello, Earthlings!" However, without an understanding of what extraterrestrial beings really are, how they function, how they travel, and how they exist, it is foolish to believe that they look, act, and respond similar to the way that humans do aside from the fact that they may look a little different.

True extraterrestrial beings may actually access our planet

through other means than just a physical spacecraft. I certainly believe there are physical beings from other planets who have visited our planet over the course of millennia, but that is a discussion for another day. However, if an alien race has mastered the astral plane and can project themselves to our planet using the power of their minds or the power of another dimension, then it is quite possible for some of these shadow people to actually be extraterrestrial beings.

Could these be some of the shorter shadow beings that have been seen? Perhaps the taller lankier ones? It's difficult to know with any certainty. Is it even possible that the shadowy nature of their physicality is actually a form of a cloaking device? Perhaps, if there is a cloaking device in place on some of these aliens it may not completely fool the human eye, and the human eye sees it as a black form, a lack of light, rather than being completely invisible.

Here's a scenario to deliberate: An alien race is searching for a new home because its planet is dying, and they have detected Earth as a hospitable planet; however, they have also detected there are intelligent beings who have already populated the planet. They decide they wish to observe the human race to determine if we are beings with which they could cohabitate, so they deploy a few of their kind on reconnaissance missions to Earth. For their own protection, they utilize a cloaking technology they've developed for their space suits and send out their emissaries. At times, these emissaries stand in the corner of people's bedrooms or in their closets or outside a window and simply observe our nature. Unfortunately, this alien race is not familiar with our physicality and how our eyes receive and translate light, so instead of humans not seeing these aliens at all, we see a dark form standing and staring at us. The cloaking device works enough in that we don't see any discernable features of the alien wearing the suit or even any features of the suit; we only see a dark bipedal form that really could be anything, but it frightens most people.

It may even be possible that what's observing us from the corner of the room is some sort of robot sent here by an extraterrestrial to observe us and not the extraterrestrials themselves. From Earth, we have sent scores of probes out into the cosmos to observe and send back information for us to study in lieu of sending humans into the depths of space. It stands to reason an alien race may do the same thing. These robots may not be a robot in which we've become accustomed in the classical sense with cogs and wheels and gears, but there's always a possibility that an advanced civilization has discovered a way to biologically create some sort of synthetic unit in the form of a biped. Perhaps that's why so many reports of grey aliens describe them all as looking very much alike. Perhaps that's also why so many shadow people tend to look very similar.

The notion that some of these entities could actually be aliens plays well into what witnesses experience during Old Hag Syndrome since there are some similarities with this phenomenon and alien abductions. Many reports of abductions include the paralysis element that most old hag reports include. Numerous abductees reported being on their backs pinned down or strapped to some sort of bed or table while being poked or prodded, so something physical is happening to them not dissimilar in fashion to the pressing down sensation old hag victims feel. Just replace the visage of the hag or ghoul with an extraterrestrial and the scenario really starts to take shape that it's an abduction and not an act of terror by a supernatural entity.

Have shadowy extraterrestrials helped with our space program? After the original publication of the second edition of this book, I was watching a presentation by Grant Cameron from the *2019 Conscious Life Expo* in which Cameron told a fascinating story originally recounted in Diana Pasulka's book *American Cosmic*. The featured individual, "Tyler D." (a pseudonym), once worked for the Space Shuttle program, and he was at a crossroads following the *Challenger* disaster while simultaneously struggling through a divorce. During this time, a general came into the offices looking for submissions of scientific experiments to be run on the Space Shuttle *Columbia*.

According to Pasulka's book, "As the general spoke, Tyler said, 'I had a memory, and it was about this experiment. I knew it would work. It was to test whether or not a noncharged material could speak with a charged material. This could only be tested in a nongravity environment. Don't ask me how I knew this would work; I just did.'"

The general, however, wasn't impressed. Tyler didn't have a Ph.D., a requirement to run the experiment, and the idea was initially dismissed. Tyler wasn't completely discouraged and got one of his colleagues who had the required Ph.D. to have the experiment performed on the Space Shuttle. If anything, they could at least publish a paper about it. To everyone's surprise, the experiment actually worked, and when the *Columbia* returned to Earth a meeting was called in Washington D.C. to discuss the successful experiment. Tyler thought he was going to be recognized with some sort of award, but what happened when a two-star general burst into the room was completely unexpected.

Diana Pasulka continued sharing Tyler's story in *American Cosmic*:

"He barked out, 'Who the hell came up with this idea?'

"I immediately stiffened with shock. The professor pointed at me. 'He did.'

"At that point I knew I wasn't getting an award. Instead, I was interrogated.

"'Where did you get that idea?' the general yelled at me.

"I could only tell him the truth, that it was a memory. That sounded like bullshit, but it was the truth. The professor confirmed it. Once the general confirmed that I was probably an idiot, he sent me out of the room. The next week at work, I was given a plaque, a patent, and five hundred dollars. I decided that week to quit my job and go into business with a surgeon buddy of mine. I decided to take my 'memory' and use it for good."

Upon learning of this story in *American Cosmic*, Grant Cameron tracked down the real Tyler D. and asked him what exactly he meant by "memory." Cameron stated in his presentation at the *Conscious Life Expo*, "He said to me, 'I'll tell you what, Grant. I woke up with that idea that one morning. I woke up with that idea in my head, and the last thing I remember from the night before is a hooded figure standing at the end of my bed.'

And I went, 'Hooded figure? Did you see his face?'

'No, I couldn't see its face.'"

If bells and whistles didn't go off for you like they did for me when I first watched this account then you must have skipped Chapter 4. Again, these dark, hooded figures seem to have a variety of functions, and I maintain that each seems to have its own individual agenda, or perhaps, there are a variety of different factions of these entities with their own agendas. This particular hooded figure seems it may have been extraterrestrial in nature, perhaps coming to Tyler D. because of his access to the space program and giving him vital information to run important scientific tests. There are many people who believe extraterrestrial races are trying to aid humanity in its advancement without publicly revealing their presence to the masses. That Tyler awoke with this information following the encounter with the hooded figure suggests a mode of thought transference or, as some have been referring to it these days, download. Again, this implies some sort of advanced knowledge or technology.

I've spoken with Grant since I watched that presentation in a quasi-interview conversation that was recorded and posted to his

Facebook page, and this is a story we talked about at length. He posed an interesting follow-up question, however: Why do so many of the shadow entities wear clothes while so many of the extraterrestrials, like the greys, run around naked? Food for thought.

I'm not saying shadow people are really extraterrestrials, but the possibility that some of them *could* be, like the hat-wearing ones Albert K. Bender experienced, is an interesting theory that's at least worth considering, especially if we agree that a "true" shadow person is an interdimensional being. We don't know with any certainty who or what can travel across dimensions, but we have to consider that there may be alien races out there from other worlds that have mastered the ability to do so. With the universe being 14 billion years old and the Earth being only 4.5 billion years old, there are likely scores of civilizations out there that have had billions of years to get a technological head start on us.

Time Travelers

One suggestion I provided for the illustration earlier in this chapter was a possible breach in time, a time displacement, or a time slip that occurred in such a way that for a brief moment a shadow and I were able to see each other, and I was able to hear its actions. If this incident had really been two moments in time catching a glimpse of each other, or echoing into each other's worlds, then it was unintentional. For this short section, we are talking about *intentional* time travel in which one being deliberately wants to access another point in time.

If we can hypothesize that some of the shadows we witness may actually be aliens using some sort of cloaking device that doesn't fully conceal themselves to our eyes, then we could also surmise the same could be true of a time traveler who uses some sort of device to move back and forth through time. Of course, this assumes there are beings, perhaps even our future selves, that possess this kind of technology, but we *are* talking about a theory here, so let's feel free to assume it. If a person in the distant future traveled back in time with the agenda to simply observe how society really operated in a remote past, they may not want to be seen and try to utilize some sort of cloaking device. It may sound redundant, but again, as with the extraterrestrials, the cloaking device in this scenario doesn't fully work and the time traveler appears as the shadow we see.

There's also another idea we can consider here. In breaching the dimension of time, the traveler may not appear fully formed on our plane of existence. Similar to what happened in the restaurant kitchen of Johnny V's, we may only catch a glimpse of a figure crossing that dimension. Some people have reported seeing shimmer-type figures, not necessarily shadows, and these may be some sort of interdimensional crossing that's being witnessed as well. Whether it's across time or some other dimension, we can't be sure, but it leaves open the possibility that some of the shadow entities witnessed could be time travelers.

In Chapter 4 of my book *Alaska's Mysterious Triangle*, I relate an experience I had while stationed at Elmendorf Air Force Base during the early-to-mid 1990s that involves shadow entities in the basement of a secure facility that could have possibly been related to time travel. I've included excerpts of it here for your consideration.

Shadows in Alaska Story

Reprinted from Alaska's Mysterious Triangle
Published in 2021 by Haunted Road Media

WWMCCS stood for World Wide Military Command and Control Systems, and during my time there we eventually became

GCCS, or Global Command and Control Systems, although the job was essentially the same but with different equipment and software. Our team was split in two, the more administrative-oriented part of the team on the top floor of the Alaskan Command (ALCOM) building and the more systems-oriented part of the team (us) in the basement. The basement was … creepy, to say the least. Our desks were located in the back corner of a large, dimly-lit room of cubicles with our supervisor's office in the very back corner, while our communications racks were in a side room with a throughway to the very back part of the Comm Center, and our massive mainframe actually sat within the Comm Center itself with its raised subfloor.

Throughout that center, but especially in that back corner office where we usually sat, something lurked. Whatever it was – or they were – was definitely shadowy in nature, many times darting behind the final partition where the extra cubicle parts were stored. Sometimes, we'd see one of these shadows dart from the room with the comm racks out the back doorway and into a small room with old servers and printers in which I'd never seen the light actually turned on the entire time I worked there. These shadows brought a dark and heavy feeling with them, but they never made any intentions known, whether sinister or otherwise. Most days, we did not see them, but there was always a dark, ominous feeling encompassing the area.

When my mother and sister came to visit during July 1995 (my father was back in Ohio breaking ground on a new house for he and my mother), I signed them in as visitors and gave them both the grand tour of the offices and the rack room. Due to security protocols, I couldn't take them into the actual Comm Center to view the mainframe. My mother, who knew nothing of the stories of the shadows which lurked within, was unnerved and completely creeped out, expressing how she definitely didn't like the feeling down in those basement offices.

ALCOM, the Colonel Everett Davis Building on Elmendorf Air Force Base (now Joint Base Elmendorf-Richardson) in January 2017. (Alvarez photo)

The story circulating the facility at the time was that the building originally opened as a hospital and our offices down in that basement had been the morgue with the room where our racks stood being the location which housed the coolers. We visualized gurneys lined up across the tiled floor with cold, dead bodies on ice where our routers, multiplexors, and patch panels were stacked up and plugged in. This, however, was just fantasy and legend. I researched the history of the building and discovered that it was built for exactly what it is being used for: command. It was never a hospital. So where did the story come from? As is human nature, it seems the story of the morgue was concocted to try to explain why we would have been seeing shadows and feeling dark and heavy presences where we worked.

Of course, plenty of skeptics have tried to state that the reason we were seeing and feeling what we did in the basement of that building was an effect due to the electromagnetic fields (EMF) of all the computer equipment, of which there was plenty. I understand that viewpoint, and on many investigations I've conducted I've ruled out the possibility of paranormal or supernatural activity due to high EMF. Exposure to unusually high EMF can create a sense of dread in a person or a feeling of being watched. However, the majority of the shadow activity that was witnessed in that computer center was in the back corner of the office area where our team sat, the furthest point you could get from all of the large electronic equipment and computer mainframes. It was actually the creepiest where there was the least amount of technology present.

When it comes down to it, I can't say for sure who or what these shadows had been. Attempting to run a paranormal investigation in a Top Secret communications center to discover the origins of shadow people wasn't going to happen, not even in the back offices. The stories that were conjured up over the years were to try to make these entities out to be the souls of people who had died in a fictitious hospital. However, since that hospital never existed and the building was only ever a command center, then from where did these shadow entities originate and why were they there? Let's explore.

The Alaskan Command building was originally built as the Colonel Everett Davis building in 1947 and was viewed as the heart of Elmendorf Air Force Base. Colonel Davis was Elmendorf's first commander and first commander of the Eleventh Air Force, establishing the original Elmendorf Army Air Field in 1940. Then a Major, Davis based himself out of Merrill Field in Anchorage that August and over the next several months established a small contingent of personnel and the Elmendorf field which saw its first plane land on November 8, 1940.

Colonel Lionel H. Dunlap assumed command from Davis shortly thereafter, and Davis remained on as Chief of Staff for Colonel Dunlap and his successor in 1942, General William O.

Butler. Davis was promoted to the rank of Colonel in June 1942, but he didn't get a chance to enjoy the promotion for very long. On November 28 that year, he and seven others perished in the plane crash of a C-47 out of Naknek to Elmendorf.

With such a tragic ending for Colonel Davis, the immediate question becomes … is he the one haunting the ALCOM building? Is it he that is possibly a shadow person many of us observed lurking about the computer center and offices? There's no reason to really believe this. While Colonel Davis certainly would have been rather attached to the Elmendorf base, the building built in his honor was constructed five years after his passing. He never stepped foot in it. So, what are these shadows?

Let's take into consideration that we're still within the confines of the Alaska Triangle and a vortex area of the Earth which wells up with energy from the magnetic core producing much of the strange phenomena experienced there. We've already discussed the concept that this vortex creates portals to other dimensions, which may very well be where missing vessels and aircraft, such as the Douglas C54-D [described in Chapter 2 of *Alaska's Mysterious Triangle*], disappear to. There are other ways in which these connections with other dimensions are witnessed and that is by the observation of shadow phenomena. I just described that above with the incident at Johnny V's in Muskogee, Oklahoma.

One other theory to consider is that these aren't really different dimensions we're looking at here as they are different points in time. Let's consider what time really is. Time is simply a human construct used to describe our reality, and it's helpful in keeping track of things like the seasons so we know when are the best times to plant and harvest crops. Oh, and your boss at work probably wants you to show up to your job at the right moment. The "river of time," however, doesn't really exist; it's just an idea we've put forth to keep track of our experience in what is really the fourth dimension. There are many who believe that all time – past, present, and future – are all happening concurrently, each moment resonating at a different frequency. However, shadow entities who are interdimensional beings are resonating on a different frequency than humans and are likely experiencing "time" differently than us.

Could the shadow entities we witnessed in the basement of the ALCOM building been an observation of a time slip powered by the Alaska Triangle? Perhaps those shadows flitting about were actually images of those personnel who had previously worked in that basement decades beforehand, shadows of real human beings living and working in another point in time. Or, perhaps, they were images of those who would come after us, some future unbeknownst to us. Could they have even been ourselves?

Astral Projections

An astral projection is an out-of-body-experience in which the participant intentionally projects his or her "astral body," light body, or soul into the astral plane, an ethereal plane of existence where one interacts with other spirit forms. Visitors to the astral plane often describe the ability to travel long distances to visit other locations around the Earth – and even the universe – in order to sight-see, learn, and visit loved ones.

Take, for instance, a grandmother who lives hundreds of miles away from her daughter and granddaughter and wishes to visit them. A physical trip isn't always feasible, but if she knows how to astral travel she may try to visit using that method just to look in on them, even if she can't interact. Imagine her projecting into their rooms at night just to simply watch them sleep, perhaps, standing in the corner of their respective rooms or even at the ends of their beds while she does so. Sounds familiar?

It's possible that some shadow entity experiences are actually astral projections of loved ones and relatives who are simply visiting at night. They could be some of the watchers standing silent and sentinel not fully manifesting because it's only their astral form in the room, essentially making them a type of *intra*-dimensional being since they're traveling within the same dimension (via the astral plane) but in a different form.

Light Beings

Graphic representation of a light being with silhouetted body.

Light beings are typically higher dimensional entities, which in some cases may be angels or spirit guides, usually appearing as pure energy. Some of these may even be human spirits who have reached a higher frequency.

We wouldn't normally associate light beings with shadow people, but take, for instance, those cases in which a person on his or her death bed has been witnessed surrounded by entities, either light or shadowy in nature. The casual observer, while initially surprised, would probably associate the light with some sort of spirit ascension into heaven or another higher plane of existence, while associating the shadow entities with … well, an afterlife journey to some place foreboding. This may not be so generalized, however.

Light beings resonate on such a high frequency that we don't usually see them, and when we do, they're typically extremely bright. But what if, they're so bright that our eyes can't correctly process what we're seeing and all we're left with is the vague, shadowy representation of a body? Stare at a lightbulb long enough and after a short while our eyes start to see the burned in silhouette image of the bulb. That doesn't mean the bulb is dark in nature.

As humans, we tend to consider things in black and white; if it's not one way it must be the exact opposite. The universe, however, is filled with gray area and plenty of in between states of being. That includes how we view the resonance of light beings.

Doppelgangers

Doppelgänger is a German word which essentially means "double walker," but when we think of doppelgängers we think of a supernatural phenomenon which has created a look-a-like version of ourselves, a copy, and in some traditions, this is an "evil twin." Do some of these apparent copies of ourselves manifest as shadow people?

Johnann Wolfgang von Goethe

There have been several famous doppelgänger sightings over the years, including an interesting case involving the famous Eighteenth Century German poet, Johnann Wolfgang von Goethe. In his autobiography *Dictung und Wahrheit*, or *Poetry and Truth*, Goethe recounted a confrontation he once had with his own doppelgänger. While traveling on the road to Drusenheim to visit a young woman with whom he was having an affair, he was distressed and lost in his own thoughts. At one point, Goethe glanced up for a moment and spotted a man dressed in a gold-trimmed gray suit. Just as quickly as Goethe had spotted the man, the man suddenly vanished. Several years later while traveling on the same road, the poet realized he was wearing the same gold-trimmed grey suit he had seen on the vanishing man years beforehand. Goethe was his own doppelgänger!

Paranormal author Meg Fisher had a doppelgänger experience at a haunted house she lived in as a child and writes about it in her book *A Haunting At 2095* under the pen name Rosella C. Rowe. One night when Meg was a teenager, she woke up to the sound of someone putting away dishes in the kitchen. She got up, walked to the hallway, and peeked out. She saw the kitchen lights were on and assumed her mother was awake and putting away the dishes. Sure enough, when Meg walked down the hall, into the family, and neared the side kitchen table, her mother walked in from the door to the garage and into the kitchen. She stopped when she saw Meg.

Meg still remembers exactly what her mother was wearing – her favorite jeans and a teal sweater – and she remembers her mother looking tired and gazing at Meg as if she didn't know who her daughter was.

Meg asked, "Mom, what's wrong?" but her mother looked even more panicked. When Meg reached out for her, her mother ran off through the kitchen and down the hall to her bedroom.

Meg ran after her and was astonished when she got to the bedroom and saw her mother sleeping in bed, wearing a nightgown. She approached her mother and tapped her on the side to wake her. The woman woke slowly, and when she did, she asked Meg if she was all right. Meg asked her mother if she'd been sleeping long, and her mother told her she'd felt sick at work, came home early, and went to bed. She'd been asleep for hours!

So … who was the doppelgänger in the kitchen that looked like Meg's mother? Was it a ghost, some sort of haunting or paranormal activity of this house? Or was it something else?

When Meg first told me this story, I immediately thought that the experience must have been some sort of time slip. For whatever reason, Meg's moment in time and her mother's – the one who was in the kitchen – crossed each other. Perhaps, this was an image from the past playing out for Meg, and for her mother, perhaps it was a glimpse into the future of her teenage daughter.

This is very similar phenomenon to what Goethe experienced in which it wasn't really a doppelgänger he saw, but it was himself years later dressed in the gold-trimmed gray suit. For some reason, he momentarily crossed paths with another point in time and was able to view an older version of himself. Is this also true of Meg and her mother, that what they experienced was actually a quick moment of time travel?

In either case, and in most doppelgänger cases, I believe, these are not manifestations of "evil twins" but are something more closely related to time slips – they just happen to be time slips of ourselves. Likewise, I also don't believe they're manifestations of shadow people, but I felt compelled to address it here since the topic of doppelgängers as possible shadow entities frequently arises during interviews and on our livestream show.

Addendum to Doppelgangers:

As new information comes to light, I'm invoking my right to change my mind, in part, on my opinion regarding doppelgängers. While I still don't believe these are manifestations of "evil twins," there may be a chance that some shadow entities are doppelgängers of ourselves within a time slip. This fascinating story was related to me when I was interviewed for Jim Harold's *Ghost Insight* podcast in November 2021.

In this account, a certain young man walked into his kitchen when he was a child and there standing near the table loomed a tall, dark hooded figure. Of course, the boy was very frightened at the imposing visage and ran off. Years later when he was much older, this same individual was standing in the kitchen at the table wearing a hoodie and making a sandwich when in the doorway he suddenly noticed the shadowy humanoid form about the size of a small child. It was then that it struck him that what he was gazing upon, and what he had seen when he was a child, was actually himself years apart. No doubt, this was some sort of time slip and what he was witnessing was a part of himself resonating across space-time, at least to a point in which he could see a shadowy form. There had been something about the conditions of those two particular moments in time, which I believe has more to do with synchronizing at a specific frequency, that his younger self was able to catch a shadowy glimpse of his older self, and his older self was able to catch a shadowy glimpse of his younger self. Call it spooky action at almost no distance, to tweak Albert Einstein's famous term.

Djinn

Djinn are pre-Islamic Arabic supernatural creatures that are generally considered trickster-type entities from some other alternative universe and have never existed on earth as humans. They are not innately good nor evil, but the more malevolent djinn have blurred the line for many as to whether or not to consider these entities as demonic. The djinn's ability to hide, conceal their true identity, and their ability to travel great distances in an instant have led many to believe that these are truly interdimensional entities that don't only roam our plane of existence but also exist in other dimensions as well.

In their book *The Vengeful Djinn: Unveiling The Hidden Agendas Of Genies*, Rosemary Ellen Guiley and Philip J. Imbrogno state they believe a number of shadow people are actually djinn. Is it possible for the dark, shadowy nature of the beings we see with our eyes and the interesting apparel some appear to wear actually be a djinn in disguise?

In their conclusions, Guiley and Imbrogno believed the form of a shadow was unnatural to the djinn entity and was more of a cover, which is conducive to the "trickster" nature of the djinn. The authors pointed to the numerous reports of the hat man and how the hats and garb the entities wear seem out of style:

> "The coat or cloak may conceal another shape. Experiencers often wonder, why the hat? That hat is usually out of style, like the mid-twentieth-century Dragnet or Dick Tracy hat [fedora], or the stovepipe hats popular in the nineteenth century. Sometimes the hat is large and floppy. We believe the hat conceals something about the entity's head – or perhaps it hides equipment."

This last remark about equipment stems from their observations that many of those who experienced shadow phenomena also had extraterrestrial experiences, and the behaviors between the shadows and extraterrestrials were similar.

Another primary reason the authors lean toward some of these shadow people being djinn is the desire of a number of these entities to strike fear into an intended victim. In Chapter 2, I talked about the hat man possibly being a type of emotional or energy vampire feeding off the fear of its victims. According to Guiley and Imbrogno, this is also, "a tactic we would expect from a djinn."

A Peripheral View

One other aspect to consider while examining the possible interdimensional implications of shadow people – the way our eyes work. Many times, when people witness shadow entities they see them out of the corner of their eyes, they get a glimpse of

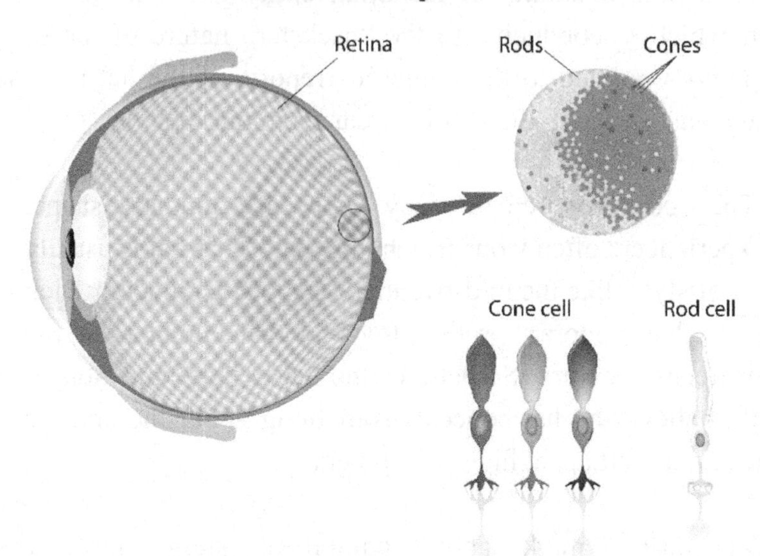

something shadowy moving about in their periphery, and when they turn to look, it's suddenly gone. Why does this seem to happen so often?

Our eyes are made up of rods and cones, the rods being low-light receptors and the cones being like the HD camera of the eye and allowing full-color, high resolution eyesight. While cones reside near the center of your retina and help you see color and fine detail, rods mostly sit away from the retina, and although you see less detail with rods, the human eye is designed as such that the faintest objects in our range of vision can be seen 16 – 20 degrees off-center. Stargazers will use a technique called averted vision, a technique in which one looks off to one side to expose the most sensitive part of the eye in order to see fainter objects in the night sky.

Seeing shadows out of the corner of the eye is such a commonly reported phenomenon that in Episode 2 of *The Shadow Dimension* docu-series, I had three different people discuss this point: Esoteric Researcher Jonny Enoch, Psychic Explorer Mark

Anthony, and Medium and Researcher Mary Marshall. Together, they painted a fantastic picture of how this works with averted vision, and in one particular quote from Mark we come to understand what we're seeing in these moments in which we glimpse the shadows in our periphery:

> "In our peripheral vision, we see slightly into the infrared range. It's like when you want to observe a comet, and if you try to look at it directly you don't see it so well. You see a comet better when you're viewing it out of your peripheral vision. Spirits, and particularly shadow people and other interdimensional beings, they're vibrating at a frequency which may be subtle. So, if you try to look at them directly you don't see it, but that's why you'll catch a glimpse of them out of your peripheral vision, because that part of your eye is more sensitive to low light. So, these entities are around us a lot, and it's learning, first off, like you, to be receptive to them, and then secondly, when you do encounter them, to learn how to observe them. Because people say, 'I thought I saw something out of the corner of my eye, and I looked at it and it vanished.' It didn't vanish."

The idea that the presence of the shadow entity may actually still be there with us when we turn to look at it may not be comforting to some, but the concept makes sense considering we know there is a world around us we cannot usually see with our range of vision. This world is composed of both physical and interdimensional elements, as well as many elements we still don't quite understand, yet it's all quite very natural.

Chapter 18

Shadow Animals

In addition to shadow people, there have been many accounts of shadow animals. Already in this book we've discussed the fascinating, yet terrifying, encounter with a dire wolf bearing down upon a woman during an Old Hag Syndrome-like attack with her husband watching in disbelief as the impressions of the massive paws pressed into her shoulders. While she could see this terrifying entity, he could not, aside from the effect it was having on his wife, making it a rather unique encounter. Other shadow animal entities are quite visible in a typical darkened form in which we usually see humanoid figures, including the shadowy images of cats, dogs, snakes, and other creatures.

Dawn Francisco had a number of shadow encounters throughout her childhood with what she has described as "shadow spiders." While one could attribute a single incident like Dawn's to a trick of the eyes, these manifestations were recurring over a number of years. The entire account is provided in *Encounters With The Paranormal: Volume 3*, but I will provide pertinent snippets of it here.

Dawn's Story

I had fallen asleep counting the beads of water that had formed on the inside of the glass. A short time later, "something" woke me up. I was still in the same position in which I had fallen asleep, so I was looking at the glass humidifier when I awoke. Only, I wasn't seeing drops of water on the inside of the glass. I was seeing tiny, fuzzy black spiders milling all about on the outside of the glass.

I bolted straight up in bed and rubbed my eyes in disbelief. Slowly, I looked over at the humidifier again only to see the spiders were now agitated and some had leapt off the glass and landed on my pillow. At that point, I started screaming bloody murder for my mom who came running into my room and flipped on the light.

The spiders simply vanished. They were just gone, and I was left clutching my blanket and sobbing. My mom told me it was the cold making me see things that weren't there, and she stayed by my side until she thought that I had drifted back off to sleep.

No sooner had she shut off the light in my room and walked out then they showed up again. They didn't appear out of thin air like magic or anything, but instead, they burst forth from my closet in a mad rush. There were hundreds of them in various sizes, from the size of a tiny thin dime to the size of a massive dinner plate. They scattered every which way, skittering up the walls all willy-nilly. They literally covered every inch of my room.

I sat upright in my bed again, clutching my blanket, fear racing through my body, my heart beating out of my chest. I was in shock and really didn't believe what I was seeing. I rubbed my eyes a few times thinking I was dreaming, but they were still there surrounding me in the darkness.

My natural defense mechanism as a small child was to start pulling all of my dolls and stuffed animals up around me kind of like a barrier. It made me feel slightly better inside, but what happened next sent my fear level to new heights.

All of those motionless fuzzy, black spiders surrounding me suddenly, in a single instant, opened their eyes … their very large, round eyes. Each piercing set of eyes were a solid deep, blood-red ruby color. All were void of any type of pupil. It was as if hell had opened hundreds of tiny windows, and I was being observed by something dark and evil.

It got worse as they all began to whisper. The sound they made resembled hissing, to an extent, yet I felt I understood in my mind what they were saying. Their message was pure evil. They had come to claim me. At that point, I wanted to sink into my bed and disappear from this horror I couldn't comprehend in my young mind.

I laid there with my eyes squeezed tightly shut until I, somehow, managed to go to sleep.

It was a couple years later after that night when the spiders opened their eyes that I came face to face with their leader. I was probably about six at the time. I look back and wonder now why their queen waited so long to show herself.

This night was different than the rest. The energy had changed. Wherein, I could always feel their presence and hear their tiny hissing whispers, this night their energy consumed me. I lay under my tent feeling overwhelmed and more uneasy than normal. Something told me, in my mind, to uncover myself, to show myself to these things. Slowly and reluctantly, I obeyed.

It felt like time had stopped as I gingerly removed my protective shield and sat upright in my bed. My eyes were drawn to the dark cavernous gaping hole of my huge double closet. Normally, I close the closet door at night hoping that would keep the spiders from emerging. But tonight, much to my horror ... I don't recall that I had left it open, so this just added to my fear.

If I strained my eyes really hard, I could detect movement from within the closet's darkness, and whatever it was it was really big, not like these tiny demons covering my walls. And then, the moment arrived.

The queen, as I called her, emerged from my closet. She was gigantic! Her massive furry body glistened like wet black crow feathers, and she had more than fifty long slender legs. Each leg had a hooked claw on the very end of it. She climbed out the of the closet and up onto the wall above, then crawled over to my door and positioned herself right above the entrance.

Well, at this point, my terror was so immense I let out a scream that I am sure all of my neighbors could hear.

My mom heard me scream, and I heard her leap out of bed and run down the hallway to my room. What happened next can only be described as something out of a horror movie. As my mom entered my room and passed underneath the doorway, the queen with great precision and timing, dropped a spider web cape that landed softly and draped itself across my mom's shoulders. She looked like some creepy bride wearing a long veil. She made her way to my bedside with the cape trailing behind her in long gauzy spider web tendrils. She was completely unaware of her ghostly attire.

I think at that moment I had a mental break. I knew there was no way I was going to tell my mom what just happened or what I was seeing. I knew that would put her over the top and she, surely, would lock me away. She sat on the bed, pulled me into her comforting arms, and asked me what was wrong. I made up something about a bad dream and that I was okay now. She kissed my cheek, covered me up, and went back to bed, all the while the queen perched above my door frame glaring at me with those piercing red eyes.

At this point, I didn't really know what to do, so I asked the queen what she wanted. I didn't ask out loud. Instead, I screamed at her in my mind.

She laughed and replied, "We want you ... We want you ... We want you!"

My heart and my soul sank through the bed, through the floor, through the earth, and dropped off into space. Never have I felt such terror and despair all at once. But I also realized that if anything was to be done about this, I WOULD HAVE TO DO IT.

The next day, I searched through my bookshelf for the Bible my grandma had sent to me. She had told me to keep it close, and when I felt frightened, I should open it to any page and there I would find a passage to help me overcome whatever was plaguing me.

So, from then on, I kept my grandma's Bible under my pillow. At night, I would no longer hide under the safety of my blanket tent. I did keep my stuffed animals and dolls around as a safety measure, though. Instead, I would lie in bed like a normal child does, but I would keep that small bible clutched in my hand, holding it close to my chest over my heart as I drifted off to sleep.

Where I have seen a form of shadow animal has been in cemeteries in the form of what I have called a shadow cat. I can't necessarily say these shadows had the distinct features of a cat, after all, it was a shadow. However, they were of the approximate size of a cat and slinked around on the ground and around trees just as felines would do.

Looking back into ancient Egyptian mythology again, there is a loose interpretation that cats were considered guardians of the underworld because of their association with the goddess Bastet. Bastet is typically depicted as a cat, herself, or as an anthropomorphic character as a woman with a cat's head. She was seen as a protector of the home, which included evil spirits and disease, and also of women's secrets. Cats were held in such high reverence by the ancient Egyptians that many of these animals were actually mummified and sometimes buried with, or at least near, their owners. Could the ancient Egyptians also have witnessed these type of shadow cats around the burials of their loved ones and deemed them guardians?

Similarly, there are many Native American legends regarding shadow animals, including the *shilombish* in Choctaw legends.

According to the Choctaw, every person has two shadows, the shilombish, or the outside shadow which always follows the individual, and the *shilup*, or the inside shadow, which after death makes a long journey westward to the Land of Ghosts. The shilombish, however, remains on Earth and can linger about the family for an extended period of time if not at rest, for instance, if the individual had suffered a tragic death or led a troubled life. This shadow could take on the form of an animal, such as a fox or an owl, and call out as these types of animals at night, disturbing the family household. The night calls are said to be that of the shilombish if there is no answering call from another animal of its own kind.

As a special addendum for the second edition of this book, psychic medium Rob Gutro has supplied a fascinating piece of work on shadow pets following up on his many years of experiences working with the spirits of animals. He's already written three volumes to his *Pets and the Afterlife* series and has expressed he may include the following piece in the fourth.

Rob's Story:

Experiences with Shadow Pets
By Rob Gutro

Pets can appear as shadows from the afterlife. To me, as a medium and a scientist, it is all about energy, and I'll explain my take on these shadow pets. This [part of the] chapter also contains my experiences with shadow pets, both cats and dogs.

I've had the gift of mediumship since I was a child, but it didn't really develop until my first dog, Buzz, was tragically killed by a car in 2005 when he was a puppy. He became the world's best canine communicator from the afterlife, and I know that he's enabled me to communicate with countless other pets in spirit. I have written three books about my experiences with pets on the other side. *Pets and the Afterlife 1*, *2* and *3* provide examples of my communications with pets on the other side and personal stories describing the many ways our spirit pets can communicate.

My Explanation on Shadow Pets

First, let me explain that I define a ghost as an earthbound entity and a spirit has crossed over into the light. They are both the result that occurs after our physical bodies die and the energy within combines with our memories, personality, and knowledge. Ghosts choose to stay behind at a fixed location of their choosing. They have limited ability to move around (but they can). Spirits, however, cross over and can appear anywhere, anytime on Earth.

Second, as energy, they require additional energy to get strong enough to make noises, touch you, move something or even show up visibly. That said, I believe that most shadows are either ghosts or spirits that don't have enough energy to appear visibly. Think of a ghost or spirit like a lightbulb that gets very little energy and appears as a dim outline.

I do think that those who are not ghosts or spirits may indeed be life from other planets in the universe, unfamiliar with our world and may react in a hostile way. Mike [has] masterfully examined those in [this] book.

My Buzz Experience

My first experience with a shadow pet occurred months after

my weimaraner Buzz passed in 2005 and after I had adopted my weimaraner, Dolly. I lived in a townhouse that had a galley kitchen and was attending to something on the counter around 9:30 PM. I thought that Dolly was sleeping somewhere in the house, and when I looked into the adjacent dining room area, I saw the backside of a weimaraner walking away from me, but the front part melted into the darkness as a shadow. I called, "Dolly," naturally thinking it was her, put down what I was doing, and followed the backside of dog down the short dark hallway that opened into the living room at the back of the townhouse. I turned on the light, and the dog was gone. I did a double take.

Knowing that the living room door to the kitchen was the only way out on the other side of the townhouse, the dog had to come back down the hallway where I was standing to get out of the room. I immediately ran upstairs to my bedroom and there, sleeping in the middle of the bed, was my (living) dog, Dolly. I then realized I had seen Buzz downstairs! Well, at least his backside was in full color, but his front half was in shadow.

My Sprite Experience

Our dachshund, Sprite, was also a rescue dog, and he was dropped into a rescue just before his thirteenth birthday. His elderly parents had passed. He was also in bad shape, and as rescuers we worked with a dachshund rescue that took him in to get him medical care. He lived until he was 16 ½ years old.

Sprite used to like to sit at our front door and just stare out the storm door window and watch people walk up and down the street we live on. He still does. Since he passed on July 8, 2013, both my husband Tom and I have occasionally seen a little Sprite-shaped shadow lying near the front door. Sprite doesn't have enough energy to appear visibly, but he wants to let us know he is still very much around our family.

My Shadow Cat Experience

As a paranormal investigator, I encountered a ghost cat in a private residence during an event. In Chapter 16 of my book *Case Files of Inspired Ghost Tracking*, I explain that a ghost cat brushed my legs as I was standing in the kitchen of the home speaking to the homeowner. When I asked the homeowner if she had ever seen a ghost cat, she acknowledged that she had. She noted seeing the cat in shadow [form] throughout the house from time to time and feeling cold sensations on her legs at night as if a cat were sitting against her.

My Shadowy Dog Experience

During a vacation in England in 2013, I saw a ghost dog as a shadow figure in an 1800s home-turned-public-museum. Sir John Soane was a famous British Architect who collected artifacts from around the world and antiquities. His home, now a museum, is filled with them for the public to now enjoy.

At the moment my husband and I opened the front door and stepped inside, I sensed a ghost, but it wasn't human. It was a dog. As we walked through the museum, I saw the ghost dog in shadow. I learned the identity of the dog as I walked through the museum when I came across a large portrait of Mrs. Soane with a little black and tan dog named Fanny perched on her lap.

I went on to learn the story of Fanny, and verified with employees of the museum that she was, indeed, running around there. You can read about the entire encounter in Chapter 18 of my book *Ghosts of England on a Medium's Vacation*.

My Franklin Experience

In 2020, our 16-year-old red, smooth dachshund, Franklin passed in May. Five months later on October 22, 2020, we had to help our weimaraner, Dolly, cross over and out of pain. She was just shy of 16 years old. As a dog dad and dog rescuer, there is nothing worse than losing your canine children.

We adopted both Franklin and Dolly when they were months old. To lose them as teenagers is devastating. To a pet parent like me, it's like losing a teenage human. Both dogs have come through to me since they passed, and each of them appeared as shadows.

Usually, a spirit will appear in places they favored in life. That could include a favorite corner of the house, a place in a kitchen where their pet bed was located, or an area where sunlight streamed through a window and onto a floor. It could be on a favorite patch of grass in your backyard, or even in your car if your dog loved car trips.

In their last year, Franklin and Dolly had beds in the kitchen because both had become incontinent, and it was easier to get them into the backyard to clean them after overnight accidents.

After Franklin passed on May 8, 2020, both my husband Tom and I saw a shadow that was Franklin's height and shape in the area where his bed had been located. We both sensed it was Franklin, and as soon as we tried to focus on the shadow, it had vanished. We realize that Franklin had just enough energy to show up to let us know he's still around.

That was just one of many ways that Franklin let us know he was around, though. In my book *Pets and the Afterlife 3*, [I included] four amazing signs that Franklin gave us within 24 hours of his passing. Months after he passed, although we didn't see him, we heard his distinct loud, sharp dachshund bark from inside of our sunporch when we and our other dogs were all outside. In fact, Franklin's bark was so loud, I actually went inside looking to see who was in the house!

My Dolly Experience

Dolly passed on Oct. 22, 2020, but she has been extremely active from spirit. In fact, she's given me so many signs and signs to friends of mine that she has quite a long chapter in the *Pets 3* book! Visually, though, I have seen her twice (so far) as a shadow and outline, sitting atop her big bed in the kitchen (it still sits there for our other two dogs). One morning, I came into the kitchen after waking at 5:30 AM as usual, and she was lying on her bed in shadow and quickly vanished. Another time, I saw her shadow on the bed during the day when I turned into the room quickly. Then she vanished. I know it takes a lot of energy to appear in full color, and one day, I know she'll be able to do it.

My Conclusion

Our pets will always be connected to us and provide many ways to let us know they will always be around (from time to time) until we cross over and meet them on the other side. When they appear as shadows, the location and shape of a shadow pet make it easy to identify which of your pets are visiting from spirit. Pets usually go to their favorite places. I've been able to identify my four dogs in spirit by keeping these things in mind, as you will be able to identify your pets in spirit.

The point of this [part of the] chapter is that our pets do come back and can appear as shadows because they lack enough energy to become fully visible. Of course, shadow appearances are just one of many ways they can let us know they're around.

Rob's experiences with shadow animals are absolutely fascinating, and it shows us that, like with human-like shadow figures, not all shadows are to be feared. Sometimes a shadow may just be a friend from our past – even a four-legged one – come to say, "Hello."

Chapter 19

Anybody Listening?

"Do shadow people have voices?" The question rang out from the back of the Assembly Theater, the site of the 2018 Ocean State ParaCon in Harrisville, Rhode Island. I was thrown off balance for a moment and my mind rifled through my mental file cabinet searching for an answer to this intriguing query. I closed the first drawer and opened the next, an immediate answer not within my grasp. So, I did what many do in such a situation and momentarily deflected while my mind continued to race.

"Is that Carl?"

Carl Johnson has received plenty of page space in this tome – and for good reason. He is a highly respected paranormal investigator and demonologist in this field, as is his twin brother, Keith, but he asked a very intriguing question which, to that date, nobody had yet asked me in all the years I'd been lecturing on the subject. *Do shadow people have voices?*

There seems to be a type of synchronicity to this world, and since then, it seems the world has been trying to provide me with an answer to that question, or at least, enough people have been recounting their experiences to me to be able to piece together some sort of adequate answer. Up to that moment, I hadn't had one person ever tell me about a voice they'd heard from a shadow person. Since then, I've had several.

The following account may sound familiar to many people who have experienced hat-wearing shadows, and I could have included this account in that chapter, but I thought it would serve this one better. Standing in the doorway of one's bedroom, in the corner, in the closet, or as in this case, at the foot of the bed, the hat man's intense aura is both mesmerizing and terrifying to his victims. I met Elina Ovcharova at the Chicago Ghost Conference, and she later recounted a number of encounters she's had with shadow-based entities, including this one with a hat man.

Elina's Story

I had a somewhat similar nightmare as I did when I was a kid, but it was much more intense. I found myself sitting up in my bed again, and I was being attacked by something I couldn't see. The window curtains were violently swaying back and forth, and I was levitating off my bed. I didn't understand what was going on, and desperate to make it stop, searched for a prayer in my head. The first one that immediately came to mind was Michael the Archangel. To my surprise, the chaos calmed down, but as soon as I looked up there was a six-foot tall solid black figure darker than the darkness in my room, wearing what looked like a hat and trench coat standing at the foot of my bed. I was in disbelief at what I was seeing. I couldn't hear him speak but I got a message telepathically saying that nobody can help me. He stood there for what felt like a minute or two longer and disappeared.

I tried to make sense of it that morning. I remembered I went to sleep with my new cross earrings that night, which I'd never done before. That and the fact it was my 23rd birthday made me wonder if that set me up for a spiritual attack. Something told me to google the hat man. What I discovered blew my mind. There was a lot that popped up about him, confirming my subconscious didn't make him up. He's usually known to stand at the foot of the bed watching you and he seems to feed off fear, which is exactly what I saw happen.

Here, again, Elina describes this hat man feeding on someone's fears, the mark of the energy vampire we discussed earlier. She also describes receiving a telepathic message, thoughts emerging in her mind that she knew were coming from the shadow entity. In this particular case, that message was rather sinister.

In Chapter 2, Cory also spoke of hearing a hat man's voice, although he couldn't specifically identify what it said. The entity just gave him a prevailing thought, which is still a form of communication. Also in Chapter 2, paranormal author Sam Baltrusis described establishing a connection with a hat-wearing shadow via thought transference and still has that connection to this day as it interferes with electronic equipment when Sam starts speaking about the being and even appears to Sam at times when he returns to Salem, Massachusetts. Elina being told by a hat man that nobody can help her is extremely specific, actual words rather than just a concept. In all of these cases, these messages were delivered to the mind via some form of telepathy, and this really makes a lot of sense considering shadow people aren't necessarily a full physical form. We don't see such things as mouths on these entities, and they may not even have vocal cords, so how would they generate an audible sound? Telepathy seems to be the more appropriate method of communication for these types of beings.

This also leads us to wonder if shadow people can also speak with other entities. If they are trying to communicate to us from their own dimension or, at least, they are trying to communicate with us in their own fashion within our own dimension, it causes us to question whether or not they can also communicate with other spirits that surround us.

Previously mentioned in Chapter 15, Shana had witnessed two "twinkle" entities following a shadow figure through a doorway and into a short passage on the top floor of the *Goldenrod Showboat*. It's unknown what was really afoot there. Were the two twinkles chasing off the shadow or were they in tandem with each other and following the shadow for some cryptic purpose (they could have been headed out to dinner for all we know). Either way, they were certainly aware of each other, and if they were aware of each other then they certainly could have been communicating with each other as well. Shana didn't hear anything with her own ears when she reached the top of the stairs and witnessed the phenomenon, but these entities could have just as easily been communicating on their own particular wavelength not audible to humans, or perhaps, there could have been some sort of telepathy performed between the twinkles and the shadow person. Again, they don't have the physical parts to act as a talk piece.

Of course, this makes it difficult for a human being to convey that they've heard messages from these entities because the voice forms in the human's mind. Thus, people get ridiculed for hearing voices. Due to the popularity of the supernatural in pop culture these days, that stigma seems to be lessening.

All of this said, I wonder if part of the reason most people haven't reported any sort of voice or communication from a shadow person is because we're simply just not listening. If their form of communication really is telepathy and most people who are encountering a shadow person are frightened at the time, then perhaps they're just too scared out of their minds within the moment to actually recognize they're being spoken to. Perhaps, their minds are racing so much that they can't receive a message from the shadow to know exactly what it's telling them or what it truly wants. In Elina's case, she did hear what it wanted, and it wasn't good, but perhaps in other cases, if we can hold back the fear of the unknown for just a brief moment, perhaps we can actually listen to what these things want, and perhaps, it's not always malicious.

PART IV

Darker Than Dark

"We filmed for four years in forty countries on six continents, and I didn't get possessed once let alone twice per episode."

—Brandy Green
Ghost Hunters International

Paranormal Panel at the Cedar Rapids
Paranormal and Psychic Expo
Cedar Rapids, Iowa
July 20, 2019

Chapter 20

The Demon Question

Are shadow people demons? I get this question all the time. Sometimes, a person will point blank tell me his or her opinion as if it's verifiable fact, "Shadow people are demons." Given everything we've covered to this point, I would be hard-pressed to make any sort of statement like that, but people are entitled to their opinions. Let's take a look at this.

When people think of demons, they immediately think of possession. We've been inundated with this notion ever since *The Exorcist* hit the silver screen and demonic possession suddenly became the primary culprit in most modern horror films, including many of the television shows depicting paranormal investigations. Demons sell, and the more times a muscular investigator gets possessed per episode the higher the ratings seem to go up. The creepier the demon looks on film, the more it resonates with us as something awful. What's more, if the demon is desecrating something we know to be innocent and good, the scarier the film tends to be.

That's why the demon nun called Valak in *The Conjuring* movie universe became so popular even though in Goetic grimoires Valak was a boy riding a two-headed dragon. The creators took the wholesome image of a nun, something we see in our daily lives as a symbol of the Church, usually an elderly woman serving soup or praying a novena for someone's health, and they completely desecrated it. Its goal: possession.

That idea that something can enter our body, take control of it, and make us do something we wouldn't normally do is extremely frightening. Back in Chapter 11, I talked about waking in the middle of the night to something pressing into me, not as if it was trying to crush me, but as if it was trying to enter me. I'll never know for sure what that was, but the idea that some other force could penetrate my body and take over for its own sinister purposes is terrifying.

Hollywood has exponentially heightened that fear, giving us grotesque imagery of possessed people hurting themselves, hurting their families, even murdering others. The entertainment value is high, but is this what really happens?

One of these movies, *Amityville II: The Possession*, was based off the work of Dr. Hans Holzer and his belief that Ronald DeFeo Jr., who committed the murders in the Dutch colonial on Ocean Avenue, was possessed when he did it. According to Holzer, this was not a demonic possession, but a possession by an angry Native American Chieftain who was gravely upset over the desecration of the lands and graves on the property. This is a hotly debated topic when it comes to the Amityville house, and that's beyond the scope of this work, but I mention it here for a couple reasons.

First of all, this suggested possession is not demonic; it's by a human spirit. An angry Native American Chieftain is certainly not a demon, and it will never become a demon. Demons are entities which never walked this earth as a human being. However, don't mistake that just because the entity isn't a demon it can't lash out and become malicious. People commonly mistake a pissed off, angry human spirit for something demonic, and I can't count how many times I've been approached by people insisting they're being terrorized by a demon because an object in their house was thrown across the room. Human spirits can throw things, too, and one term for the misguided assignment of blame to a demon in which paranormal activity may or may not exist is *parapsychological projection*. Humans tend to fear what they don't understand, and when it comes to paranormal activity, there seems to be a fear-based kneejerk reaction to call every little thing that happens demonic.

Secondly, Holzer prefaces his book, *Murder In Amityville*, with a discussion about possession and briefly touches on what we've been calling Old Hag Syndrome:

> "The word possession comes from the Latin possedere, which means, quite obviously, 'to possess, to own, to take over.' Taking the word's two components, however, we find possession consisting of post and sedere. The latter word means 'to sit, to be situated,' and the 'post' generally stands for 'after' or 'beyond.' Thus, when we translate freely, possedere means 'to sit on top of.' It is interesting to note in this connection that in the Middle Ages, a popular conception of possession included a wraith or gnome sitting on top of the possessed individual, pushing down upon his or her body, causing nightmares and other forms of altered states of consciousness. The concept of the word possession indicates that it relates to a total takeover, and total control of an individual by another individual or some outside force. Possession excludes the will of the possessed. It presupposes the inability of the victim to overcome the attacking force and in submitting to it, becomes its tool."

In all of this sitting, pressing, and possessing, Holzer never mentioned the word demon. He does talk about the offending entity being a wraith or a ghoul, and we even saw earlier in this book a case in which a dire wolf was involved, yet none of these are termed demons. So, if many of these negative entities aren't actually demons, then what exactly *is* a demon?

In his book *Shadow Realms: Demonology Handbook* which he co-authored with Lana J. Brock, demonologist Carl Johnson defines for us:

> **Demon** – The umbrella term for malicious spirit entities which seem intent on plaguing living, human beings and turning us away from God, or inflicting as much torment as is within our means. It is supposed that demons are invariably hostile and resentful yet also fearful, for they are aware of their ultimate fate: their inevitable disposition at Judgment Day.

Carl and Lana wrote 300 pages on the topic of demons, and others have written significantly large tomes on the subject as well, so this chapter is not going to be a complete understanding of everything regarding demons. I think the important takeaway here is a basic understanding of what these entities may or may not be since popular culture has done an amazing job of muddying those waters.

Inhuman. This is a term that is bandied about quite often when discussing demons, and we hear it defined with trembling and fear in the films. Inhuman simply means it never walked the earth in human form, but let's take it a step further. In speaking with demonologist James Annitto, a Deacon in the Catholic Church, he explained further, "Demons, by Christian definition, are considered to be angels that have fallen from the grace of God through their jealousy of man. These beings are considered inhuman, as they have never known a physical life. They are pure spirit in form, just as their angelic counterparts are pure spirit in form."

Oppression. With such a focus on possession in film, television, and pop culture, as discussed above, oppression often gets overlooked, but in reality, is more common than possession, often a precursor to the latter. Carl Johnson tells us in more detail in *Shadow Realms*: "When someone rather suddenly and inexplicably becomes anti-social, withdrawn and preoccupied with dark and negative interests, or abandons many previous interests, they could be exhibiting symptoms of demonic oppression which can also be referred to as demonic infestation. This may be co-symptomatic of clinical depression and distinguishing one from the other is difficult, especially in the early stages. A decided avoidance of sunlight, bright lighting, normal social interaction, a noted aversion to religious objects such as the Holy Bible and especially negative and irrational reactions to discourse on spiritual matters are indications (not proof) that something demonic has come into play."

I appreciate that Carl included the phrase "not proof" in that last statement since, all too often, people will take a single moment in time and jump off the deep end with it. I don't want to come off as dismissive. After all, some of these things are scary as hell. However, we need to be careful about what we label as demonic. I've had someone tell me before she *knew* she had a demon, and when asked how she knew, her explanation was that a candle had flown off the mantle over her fireplace one night. As stated previously, human spirits can throw objects, too, so how do we know what's demonic and what's not?

Deacon James Annitto weighed in on this: "Demonic activity can manifest in many ways, but we must be careful in labeling entities as demonic. Psychologically speaking, the power of suggestion is quite powerful, and using such a label can lead a person down a much darker path, unnecessarily. Any suspected demonic activity needs a thorough analysis on many levels before it can be deemed demonic or otherwise. The case must be analyzed on a spiritual level, as well as psychologically, medically, and scientifically. Quite simply; not all things that go bump in the night are demonic."

Do I think all shadow people are demons? No. Do I think *some* shadow people *could* be demonic? Yes, some shadow people could be a demonic infestation, and I've already described at length in this book the case in Edmond, Oklahoma, with the red-eyed shadow figure that was eventually deduced to be demonic by a demonologist with decades of experience: Carl Johnson.

Here's the thing – it took us a half dozen initial investigations, a bevy of follow-ups, and all the days Carl was involved to finally label the entity with red eyes a demon. The depiction on *The Haunted* television show is that we investigated once, got a nasty EVP (electronic voice phenomenon) recording, and called in Carl. That's far from what happened, but the production company only had 42 minutes to tell their story. This is where television and pop culture does us a great disservice. While I believe the proliferation of paranormal television shows has done a fine job in allowing experiencers to become more comfortable in coming forth and telling their stories – it's not as taboo as it was in the mid-1900s – the focus on entertainment and jump scares has led to the dissemination of poor, and often inaccurate, information. There's not a demon lurking around every corner like Hollywood leads us to believe.

In *Shadow Realms*, Carl Johnson and Lana Brock each take a chapter to break down *parapsychological projection*, but I really appreciate a warning Ms. Brock gives:

> "Too many of the 'would be' ghost hunters or self-labeled demonologists jump the gun and play with the lives of real people by not conducting thorough pre-investigative interviews with the client and their family. If something critical were to come about to cause the client to become

> emotionally injured, disgruntled, or offended, this could backfire against the investigator or demonologist. … What we do will impact the client and influence them. Paranormal/Demonic investigations, cleansings, and exorcisms are a serious matter not to be trifled with; and neither are the lives of the clients involved."

We were extremely careful in that Edmond case, proactively responsible as we thoroughly investigated and researched over several months, deducing what exactly we were dealing with before Carl was called into the case to help. New information was still forthcoming even within days of the cleansing night, all of which was important to how we proceeded. You can never have too much information, especially when dealing with a nefarious dark entity that is disrupting an entire household.

Chapter 21

Are They Evil?

Are shadow people evil? This question alone has so many varying answers within the paranormal field that it bears more scrutiny than it probably ought. Scores of people have reported being terrorized by shadow people while others have simply observed the presence of one. Take into consideration that this type of supernatural phenomenon is its own entity, its own "life form," so to speak, and no, they're not evil ... and, yes, they are.

I've read and heard some individuals call shadow people the evilest of all things that are evil, the darkest of the dark, and that may be true in some cases. As previously discussed, the hat-wearing entities and the shadow figure with red eyes seem to take pleasure in terrorizing their victims. They may even bring an entourage with them to partake in whatever nefarious deeds they're up to in order to frighten and torment. Some people report an oppression while others report physical harm at the dark hands of these shadow entities.

Yet, there are other reports of shadow people that seem far less invasive and even rather passive. Those shadow forms that peer in at you from a doorway, while perhaps voyeuristic and slightly creepy, are not doing anything harmful and are rather benign. The wisp I saw dart away from me at Johnny V's acted far more in the fashion that I had scared *it* rather than something that was looking to do me harm. And there are some shadow people that seem to have no idea you're even present as it passes down a hallway or through an open door, oblivious to everything else while it walks or floats by.

With the varying types of interaction between shadow people and humans, both harmless and harmful, I contend that shadow people can be both good and evil. I don't believe in an all-inclusive "shadow people are evil" stance that some have proliferated. I believe shadow entities are just like humans in the regard that they each have their own agendas that drive their actions and cause them to act out against us ... or not. Some seem to simply be observing us, some seem to have no idea we're even present, and yes, some seem to wish to harm us, even feed off us, perhaps. As with humans, they each seem to have their own motivations that we could classify into what we call good and evil.

At the risk of sounding overly-simplistic, I offer the following: Some people are good. Some people are bad. Some shadow people are good. Some shadow people are bad. There's a lot of gray area in between, too, and like humans, shadow people have a variety of motivations that make their interactions with our world and the people in it very situational.

My Edge of the Rabbit Hole livestream co-host, Victoria Mundae, has operated tours of and has investigated historic Old Town Spring, Texas, many times and has experienced several shadows there. Some of these shadows were certainly dark and ominous; however, she has also experienced a shadow entity there, possibly the area's famous "headless engineer" spirit, who is more friendly and helpful in nature. The following is an excerpt from an interview I conducted with Victoria for *The Shadow Dimension* docu-series describing this incident at the historic icehouse in Old Town Spring.

Victoria's Shadow Dimension Zoom Interview

November 24, 2020

I feel that it is possible to build a relationship with a shadow person. When I was doing the ghost tours out in Old Town Spring, they would always tell me when you're done with your tour come on over and you can do the investigation with us.

Old Town Spring was basically just a stop on the road, really where the railroad workers would stay when they were actually building the railroad. Of course, they had places where they would camp, and there were a couple of small buildings. There was one building that was really, really well-constructed right close to the railroad tracks, and that was actually the kitchen.

So, part of the investigation that we would do is we could actually go into that building because it was always repurposed. First, it was the cookhouse, and then it became an icehouse after the railroad was finished. And of course, it being the wild west town, it kind of became the morgue, too. They would put people on ice.

So, I was in the icehouse with the girl who was leading the investigation. We were out there at midnight, and you could hear somebody walking around the icehouse. We could hear somebody walking around out there. We were away from everybody else. There was nobody else in that town. And so, we were standing there with all of our tools and everything, and the light broke. So, I naturally looked over, and I saw a shadow go by. I said, "There's somebody out there."

[The girl leading the investigation said], "Nope. Nope. There's nobody out there."

Sure enough, it came around to the other door and the light broke again. I looked over there, and was like, "Okay there is somebody over there." So, I ran outside and I was looking for someone, because there is no way – it's gravelly over there, it's part of the railroad – and I could hear someone walking on the gravel. Very distinct. Very loud. Like a large heavy man. [But] there was nobody around. I ran to the other side. There was *nobody* around. You could tell if somebody was there because there's no place to go, really.

I came back in and I said, "Ok, there's somebody out there, but I don't know who it was." A few minutes later it went by again. "Oh my God, he is so tall! Did you see him that time?"

She said, "Yeah, I saw him that time."

I said, "He's so tall. I can't even see his head!"

He reminded me of my grandpa. My grandfather was huge, huge, huge. He was a welder and he wore overalls, and that's what the shadow man had on. You could just tell that he had overalls on by the way he was shaped.

We would go to other parts of the town, and you could hear him walking. Then you would see shadows on the buildings, but nobody is out there. So, I would say, "Maybe he's like my grandpa and is just going to protect me."

So, whenever I would walk around on these investigations – one, two, sometimes three o'clock in the morning – just a handful of us little gals out there with our equipment, I felt like he was protecting me, kind of. There was one night I was leading a tour, and we were going to go in the icehouse – pitch black, dark moon, can't see anything – and I start to walk in, and something hits me on top of the head. I just knew I walked into a board or something. So, I bent over, and I might have said an expletive or something, and I stood up looking for the boards when a man behind me said, "You almost walked into that spider web."

It was a huge spider web across the door with a big ol' spider! So, I'm quite confident it was him, the headless engineer, who was protecting me.

Not the "headless engineer" but one of the other shadow entities routinely seen around Old Town Spring, Texas.

(Photo courtesy of Victoria Mundae)

So, why have all shadow people been labeled "evil" by many of the so-called "experts" out there? Why does their entire race get stereotyped? People fear what they don't understand, and shadow entities are certainly a realm of supernatural creatures and phenomena which we don't understand. Even as I write this tome that is in your hands, the amount of information you're receiving about these entities is really just the tip of the iceberg. There is far, far more we need to research and learn about these beings before we can truly fathom some sort of real understanding about who or what they are. Therefore, because *some* of these entities have been up to something malevolent and they're of a dark color, due to our lack of understanding, they *all* get lumped into being malevolent in nature.

Poor shadow wisp at Johnny V's who fled at the very sight of me. I bet he never knew he was the fearsome scourge of the paranormal realm that could have risen to great heights within that kitchen and slammed me to the floor, sucking the very essence of my soul from my body as I writhed and became no more. I suppose some might say it was a missed opportunity by this shadow person, that I caught him off guard, and on a different day I would have suffered its wrath. Perhaps. Or, perhaps not.

While at first Tammy Hayn back in Chapter 4 thought the dark hooded figure she witnessed repeatedly drifting from her bedroom into her son's room while he suffered medical issues was there to pass him over to the other side, she ultimately believed the entity was there to help the child through that time of his life. She also believed that while she couldn't see it at the time, the entity actually whispered into the ear of the doctor to run different tests that ended up saving the boy's life. How could something so benevolent like that possibly be evil?

For myself, I have to think back to that very first shadow person interaction I had in my bedroom and reevaluate. Was it really trying to do something evil and nefarious? Think about what it really did. First, it observed me from the corner of my bedroom. While certainly creepy, that's not necessarily evil. It then approached my bed and leaned over me. Again, that's still pretty creepy, but it's still not necessarily evil. It then took hold of my arms and crossed them over my body. Ok, now my personal space has been invaded. A line has definitely been crossed. But was I being harmed? Was I in pain? Being a child, I was absolutely terrified, so much to the point that my mouth gaped open and nothing would come out no matter how hard I tried. Yet ... there actually was no pain. I wasn't actually being harmed. The entity then suddenly darted off down the hall and plunged into a closet. That was it. I then found my voice and legs and ran screaming to my parents' room. So, what the heck really happened?

For years, I lived with the fact that this thing had terrified me. Of course, it had. At the outset, when it stood in my bedroom corner, I thought there was an intruder in the house set out to murder me. I'd seen enough television and movies by that age that I knew what happened if you awoke to someone standing in your corner. You'd have just enough time to gasp before your throat was slit or a pillow was shoved over your face. But that didn't happen. It did physically interact with me, but this interaction was some strange crossing of my arms across my body, not the plunging of a murderous knife into my chest. What did this crossing of my arms mean before it ran off down the hall?

It wasn't until a few years ago in 2016, when describing this incident to psychic medium Tracey Lockwood as a guest on her radio show that the idea of a non-threatening action of this shadow person was introduced. Tracey suggested that this entity may have, for whatever reason, thought I was dead and proceeded to put my body into a burial pose. The vision she had in her mind of the arms crossed over my body was that of effigies on Egyptian mummy sarcophagi holding the crook and flail (this depiction was also used on statues and other artwork). This was an intriguing notion. Could

Canopic coffinette of King Tutankhamen discovered in his tomb with three others that each held his internal organs. The way King Tut is shown here holding the crook and flail is a little lower across his body than where the humanoid shadow person had pulled my arms but is still in very similar fashion.

Photo by: D. Denisenkov, 2012
Wikimedia Commons

this being really have seen me lying there, thought I was dead, tried to put me into a proper burial position, and when it finally noticed me trying to scream it fled, perhaps in fear, down the hall? If that idea were true, it would completely negate the premise that this thing was doing something harmful to me, would eliminate the likelihood it was evil, and could even cast it in a light that it was doing something ... well, honorable. What a twist!

A few months later another person who had not heard the broadcast with Tracey offered up the same suggestion. I had been telling this story for years, and no one had ever suggested a less-than-malevolent proposition for the shadow person's actions, and now there were two. I had to consider it, and in doing so I had to place myself back into my eight-year-old body, back in the bedroom in Westfield, Massachusetts, back in that bed that had been my nighttime sanctuary until I graduated high school and left for basic training in the United States Air Force. The covers were pulled up to my chin, the sheet my small fingers played with, much like I'd do with the pillow case while I simultaneously sucked my thumb when I was four, and the thin blue bedspread that retained my body heat. I was lying down on my back, my black, moppy hair already contorted in 2,100 different directions from tossing around in my sleep, and my eyes fluttered opened. And there it was.

I didn't try to scream this time. I was now an adult viewing the situation. I wasn't physically there, but I was projecting my adult self into a memory from my childhood — not a dream — a memory. There it stood in the corner between the window on the far wall that overlooked the driveway and the closet on the adjacent wall, sentinel and silent. I stared at it, and it stared at me. I didn't scream this time, I just observed it, much like it had observed me over 35 years beforehand. It looked like a human figure, but it wasn't. There were no features, no face to speak of, no hair, no clothing. Nothing. That was probably the most unsettling aspect, that a figure so familiar contained nothing with which to identify it.

It then approached the bed and leaned over me. There was no sound. It was as silent as the night itself, almost as if it were a part of it. There were no footsteps, no creaking floors, no rustling of clothes. Nothing. Even when it leaned over me there was no sound of breath — if it had a nose or mouth it didn't expel or inhale air through either one. And I didn't feel the heat of its breath on me. Did this thing even require breath? Was oxygen not an issue?

It then took my arms, rather, it grabbed me by the wrists —

what did it feel like? It simply felt like someone – anyone – was taking hold of my wrists. Just like that. There was no electric feel, there was no immediate feeling of dread, there was no sudden chill. It was as plain as anyone else taking hold of my wrists and crossing my arms across my body, as if they were human hands. I felt my flesh rub together, the midpoint of the crossing and the bend of my elbows on the upper part of my chest not far from my neck. As a child, my mouth gaped open to scream, but nothing came out. As an adult, I just simply observed, and I observed this shadow entity turn from me and run out the door down the hall. I craned my head to watch it. It had legs and feet, I could tell it was running, but it was so amazingly quiet. I did not hear any footfalls at all. It then turned to its right, opened the closet door, and disappeared inside, closing the door behind it. So, this was before my father had transformed our once long bathroom into two smaller ones, eliminating that closet and building a new one at the end of the hall. That was it. It was gone.

Was that evil? I don't believe so. I'll probably never know the true intentions of this shadow person, but looking back now through adult eyes I don't see much of anything malicious in these actions, and the idea this entity may have seen me as dead, perhaps because I was lying on my back, seems a bit more plausible. By simply changing the perspective and offering an alternative viewpoint, this malevolent being now becomes, first respectful then, secondly, frightened.

As a follow-up in May 2021, I underwent a hypnotic regression by hypnotherapist Arianna Corsino who specializes in past life regression and quantum healing and trained under Delores Cannon. There were many things we covered in our session, but one thing I specifically wanted more answers to was my childhood bedroom incident with the shadow entity – and answers I got, although they lead to even more questions.

During this hypnosis session, I actually became the shadow

entity. I could see the entire bedroom from its perspective, and I could see my small eight-year-old body lying in the bed. What was difficult to look at was the sheer fright in the face of the child, his mouth was open, desperately trying to scream, but the poor little boy just couldn't. What's interesting, is that the emotions I started feeling were not mine as Michael, they were coming from the shadow entity. It wasn't there to do me harm. It didn't even realize I could see it until I started reacting, and it felt terrible that it had frightened me so much. So, it approached my bed, crossed my arms across my body as a sort of self-hug, patted me on the wrists in a comforting gesture (that was new), and then tore off down the hall to get out of there. What a different perspective I had just witnessed!

Since there was engagement with the entity during this session, Arianna began asking it questions, such as what it was doing in the bedroom. It answered that it was simply there to observe and study humanity, that it was curious about our species. It had traveled there from a great distance, and what I had seen wasn't what it really looked like. Arianna then followed up and asked about where it came from, was it from another dimension? The entity responded that we might call it another dimension, but really it was from another "space."

What the difference is between another dimension and another space, I'm not yet quite sure, but this information is certainly helpful for my ongoing research at The Connected Universe Portal. The big take away here, of course, for this chapter is that this shadow person was not there to do me harm. It was not evil.

From where does this persistent idea come that all shadow people must be evil? Perhaps the easiest answer is to simply say people fear what they don't understand. This is true, and we certainly don't seriously understand what shadow people really are even though we have our theories – and I've spent an entire book covering the topic.

There seems to be an innate human trait to fear the dark, whether that be a dark room, the darkness of the night, or things that are dark in nature. People who actually enjoy these things are usually seen as eccentric (at best) or strange (at worst). While so many other species are nocturnal and venture out at night, using the darkness to cloak themselves from would-be predators, most humans prefer the light to be left on so they're not left to wonder what may be lurking in the shadows – perhaps a shadow, itself. In popular culture, our horror movies are generally dark and brooding. Even a look at ancient texts as we did earlier, shows a fear of the dark.

Professor Tom Shippey in his book *The Road To Middle-Earth* describes J.R.R. Tolkien's viewpoint of shadow and how he used it in his modern-created mythology, *The Lord Of The Rings*:

> Do shadows exist or not? It is an ancient opinion that they do and they don't. In the Old English poem *Solomon and Saturn II* the pagan Saturn asks the Christian Solomon (he *is* a Christian in this text) 'what things were that were not?' The answer is oblique, but it contains the word *besceadeð*, 'shadows'. Shadows are the absence of light and so don't exist in themselves, but they are still visible and palpable just as if they did. That is exactly Tolkien's view of evil. Accordingly Mordor is 'Black-Land', 'where the shadows lie', or even more ominously 'where the shadows *are*' (my italics); Aragorn reports that 'Gandalf the Grey fell into shadow'; Gandalf himself says that if his side loses, 'many lands will pass under the shadow'.

While Professor Shippey may be examining a fictional text, his examination includes, at length, the influence of ancient mythology on a more modern literary work, and we see that Tolkien incorporates those ancient concepts fairly seamlessly. After all, the land of Mordor is where "the shadows lie" and is the dwelling place of the dark lord, Sauron. Also, Tolkien's legendary Ringwraiths mix shadows with ghostly apparitions, although those apparitions can really only be seen when Frodo wears the magic ring of darkness. The point is that much of our ancient mythology depicts shadow as evil, and Tolkien extended that concept into what is, arguably, the most popular modern mythology. Even the recent television phenomenon, *Game Of Thrones*, based on the *A Song Of Fire And Ice* novels by George R.R. Martin, played on this with one of its many iconic lines, "For the night is dark and full of terrors." But, is it accurate?

I believe we can also look at ancient mythology and see that it doesn't always agree that all shadows are evil. We saw earlier with the Egyptian *khaibit*, that they believed this was one of seven parts of the human soul, a shadow left to linger on earth. The Greek *shades* were also human souls who needed to pay the ferryman, Charon, to crossover into the underworld or they would be left to wander the earth as ghosts. These entities in mythology are certainly not the evilest of all things that are evil. They simply exist.

I'm not trying to minimize the experiences people have had with shadow people – some of these interactions are legitimately frightening. However, there's much more going on here we need to understand.

We humans crave for black and white. What's yes and what's no? Don't leave me guessing. Having simple facts allows us to make quicker decisions, solutions are easier to figure out, and you're not left wondering if you made the right choice. From the mundane daily options of figuring out what's for dinner to picking the right stock to play, it would all be easier if it was as black and white as, "We're having Mexican tonight," or "I'm investing in Apple." If only life were so simple. Usually, it plays out more like, "Well… I don't know if I'm in the mood for Mexican, maybe

Italian. No, that's too carby." And, "Apple has always been a good company, but I don't know if they'll get enough sales with the latest iPhone. Plus, past performance is never an indicator of future…" And on and on.

Our world is a lot of shades of gray, and I imagine the world of the shadow people is much the same. We share the same universe, after all – it's all connected, even from our dimension to theirs. So, while there are certainly terrifying experiences with shadow entities that are serious cause for concern, there are others just as mundane as passing your neighbor on the sidewalk. It's just that this particular neighbor happens to be a shadow.

(NOT SO) FINAL THOUGHTS

The Miriam-Webster dictionary lists 14 varying definitions for the word *shadow*, and provides the following as the second:

shadow: partial darkness or obscurity within a part of space from which rays from a source of light are cut off by an interposed opaque body

Our vision works when light rays reflect off an object and enter our eyes, but if light rays don't reflect off an object then we don't see it. According to the definition above, a shadow cuts off those rays from the light source, and there is no reflection into our eyes. Thus, all we see is that blackness. Are we unable to see what these shadow figures truly are simply because they don't reflect light? Do they absorb the light when it hits their bodies, or does something else happen to it? These are some of the most unusual types of beings that we know about in our world today, yet we only know scant fragments about them

Earlier in this book we talked about the black smoke or mist witnessed at the House on Round Top Farm, also known as *The Conjuring* House (the Perron house), and some of the amazing activity that happens there, but we've barely covered a pinprick of all that has happened there over the centuries. Something routinely observed at the house is the sensation that time seems to stand still, even for the spirits. There are accounts of apparitions appearing there and looking at the living as if the living were the ones that had been the ghosts. Author and former farmhouse resident, Andrea Perron, likes to say that time doesn't exist at the farmhouse, that it's a portal cleverly disguised as a farmhouse, and she offers up this wonderfully eloquent description in the first volume of her *House Of Darkness House Of Light* trilogy:

> The farmhouse had a life of its own. Its doors were not simply wooden and hardware barriers between rooms. They were passages between dimensions; the form and function of time travel. Each door in the house was a portal to the past and future, as well as present, but they were also utilized as an overt method of communication; for the pronouncement of a presence. The spirits were all perfectly capable of coming and going without the benefit of doors and windows. They often walked right through them, especially the children. None requiring anything tangible to make a grand entrance, their presence alone was enough to capture the attention of any mortal and yet, the wrought iron latches would mysteriously lift, creaky doors would slowly open, as if for dramatic effect. Click.

We don't know why these entities act the way they do, what their purpose may be, and what it is that brought them to our world. We theorize. We speculate. We assemble the data we've collected and try to make sense of it. Some try to suggest their spirit guides have given them the answers about shadow people, and while I believe spirit guides exist, I think they have more important things to do than to define shadow entities to a select person or two. Others, yet, have cast shadow people as the evilest of all entities, the darkest of the dark, injecting fear into the subject and a type of shock value we typically find on over-the-top, heavily dramatized paranormal television shows. We simply just don't know for sure what these things are, and while exercising a degree of caution is prudent, immediately dragging an exorcist into the situation is probably a bit much if that shadow was just Grandma Trudy trying to manifest and say, "Hello."

For me, when it comes down to it, I believe there are a variety of entities in this universe which take on the form and shape and color of some sort of shadow. I believe a true shadow person is an interdimensional being, however there are many other entities that take on the characteristics of a shadow entity, much like sports players suiting up in similar uniforms yet having many differences. The Red Sox are different from the Yankees, as a pitcher is different from a catcher, as a large, power hitting first baseman is different from a slender, slick-fielding shortstop. The positions, sizes, and skills are all vastly different, as are the differences between the personalities of each individual player, yet they all wear similar laundry.

However, the one that is the true, legitimate shadow entity, the absolute real deal, is from another dimension entirely – call it *The Shadow Dimension* – crossing into our realm for a brief moment to interact with us, observe us, or to have some other purpose entirely, and we happen to stumble upon it, sometimes while waking, sometimes while sleeping, sometimes while walking into a kitchen or unpacking boxes.

This is a fascinating subject we'll continue to study, make mistakes, and reassess in an ongoing pursuit of the unknown. Shadow people aren't just a mystery of this world, they're a mystery of this universe, and we'll keep exploring the vast reaches of time and space to make new discoveries about these strange, esoteric entities in the years to come.

Continue to walk with me…

CONTRIBUTORS

SAM BALTRUSIS

Sam Baltrusis, author of *Wicked Salem: Exploring Lingering Lore and Legends*, has penned more than a dozen paranormal-themed books including *Mass Murders: Bloodstained Crime Scenes Haunting the Bay State*. He has been featured on several national TV shows including the Travel Channel's *A Haunting*, *Most Terrifying Places*, *Haunted Towns*, and *Haunted USA*. In 2020 he made cameo appearances on several television programs including *Paranormal Night Shift*, *Hotel Paranormal*, and *Forbidden History*. Baltrusis is a sought-after lecturer who speaks at libraries and paranormal-related events across the country. You can find his work at www.sambaltrusis.com

BRITTNEY CRABB

Brittney Crabb has been recounting her paranormal experiences and sharing in her investigative adventures for over a decade on her brittyy44 YouTube channel (which can be found at http://www.youtube.com/brittyy44), as well as narrating ghost stories from around the world in very stylish fashion.

Cory Davenport

Cory Davenport is the Managing Editor of *The Sunken Press*, an independent news outlet focused on solving issues through education and boosting community members with important missions. Previously, Cory was a reporter for the *Alton Telegraph* and Riverbender.com.

Jonny Enoch

Jonny Enoch is a clinical hypnotherapist, lecturer, and writer from Vancouver, BC, Canada. Not only has he been researching extraterrestrial phenomena and esoteric subjects for over 20 years, but after witnessing a series of unexplainable events while growing up, his search for answers has led him on adventures all over the world. This includes interviewing ET contactees, whistleblowers, and UFO witnesses. You can find his work at www.metaphysicalsource.com

Cathy E. Gasch

Cathy E. Gasch is the author of *My Life Amidst The Paranormal*. She was born, raised, went to school, worked and still lives in the state of Maryland. Most of Cathy's leisure time is spent reading and researching family history as well as historical locations. She loves to travel and has been to Ireland, Scotland, England and many wonderful and fascinating places in the United States. Cathy's paranormal experiences have spanned over 50 years, and through them, she continues to learn about herself and the world, often times, through the eyes of those who have passed on.

Eric Girard

Eric Girard is self-employed at PrintablePartyZone at Etsy.com and has been a party and wedding graphic designer since 2014. He is the owner and founder of RIParanormal (Rhode Island Paranormal), established in 2007, and does everything from investigating to operating the team Facebook page to editing the videos for the team's YouTube channel (RIParanormal The RIPple Effect). RIParanormal is also a part of the Rhode Island Chapter of The North American Dogman Project. Additionally, Eric is also a huge horror movie collector.

Rob Gutro

Rob Gutro is an author, paranormal investigator and medium with Inspired Ghost Tracking of Maryland. Since he was a child, he could receive messages from ghosts or spirits (who have crossed over). He connects with people and pets who passed, and has become known as a "pet medium." He wrote the books *Pets and the Afterlife*, *Pets and the Afterlife 2*, *Ghosts and Spirits* and *Lessons Learned from Talking to the Dead*, *Ghosts of England on a Medium's Vacation*, and *Kindred Spirits* to teach others how ghosts and spirits communicate with the living and to give proof of the afterlife (available on Amazon.com). He has also contributed to Mike Ricksecker's *Encounters with the Paranormal* series. As a scientist, he also provides some scientific explanations about how energy is the baseline for the afterlife and the medium that entities use to communicate. He can be reached at www.robgutro.com

Carl Johnson

Carl Johnson has been exploring unexplained phenomena since the age of 17. He specializes as a demonologist, was a member of The Atlantic Paranormal Society for eight years, and appeared on the first two seasons of the popular SyFy Channel series *Ghost*

Hunters. Carl has also been featured on the Animal Planet series, *The Haunted* and Travel Channel's *Most Terrifying Places in America* and *Ghost Adventures*. He is a founding member of the Order a Selohaar, dedicated to martial practice, researching history, chilvalric ideals and the Carcosan system. Carl also organizes the Ghost Tours at historic Slater Mill, and the H.P. Lovecraft Commemorative Activities Committee.

Keith and Sandra Johnson

Keith and Sandra are co-founders of New England Anomalies Research and host a local TV talk show dealing with paranormal topics called Ghosts R N.E.A.R. which airs locally in Rhode Island and can also be seen online. Keith has been featured on the SciFi channel's *Ghost Hunters* as a consulting demonologist, and both he and Sandra are former core members of The Atlantic Paranormal Society (TAPS). They have been featured as demonology consultants in two first season episodes of the A&E series *Paranormal State* as well as assisting with documentaries dealing with the paranormal, including *Haunted R.I.* and New Gravity Media's *14 Degrees*. Keith is also the author of the *Paranormal Realities* book series that chronicles his experiences as a paranormal investigator.

Meghan Talbert:

Originally from NJ, Meghan currently resides in Maryland with her husband and two children. Meghan has always had an interest in the paranormal since a young age and has formally been a paranormal investigator for ten years. The experience shared in this story is one of the reasons Meghan pursued the paranormal field.

Special Thanks also to:

Shana Wankel, Shawn Gilmore, Tonia Sargisian, Cory Davenport, Michelle LeBaron, Tammy Hayn, Tonya Hayn, Lacye Lembke, Cory and Jennifer Heinzen, LulyTubee, Sierra Huber, Dawn Francisco, Elina Ovcharova, and James Annitto

Those assisting with *The Shadow Dimension* project mentioned throughout the second edition of this book Carl Johnson, Keith Johnson, Elise Giammarco Carlson, Andrea Perron, and Dave and Donna Nunnally of It's Raining Zen, Mark Anthony, Sam Baltrusis, Jonny Enoch, Corey Heinzen, Mary Marshall, Victoria Mundae, Coyote Chris Sutton, and Nicole Guillaume.

BIBLIOGRAPHY

Arabi, Shahida. "7 Ways Emotional Vampires Drain Empaths And Highly Sensitive People." *Thought Catalog*. Accessed at https://thoughtcatalog.com/shahida-arabi/2018/03/7-ways-emotional-vampires-drain-empaths-and-highly-sensitive-people/

Bostrom, Nick. "Are You Living In A Computer Simulation?" *Philosophical Quarterly* (2003) Vol. 53, No. 211, pp. 243-255. Accessed at: https://www.simulation-argument.com/simulation.pdf

Braden, Gregg, writer, performer. "Evidence Of Our Simulated Reality." *Missing Links*, season 2, episode 1, Feb. 8, 2018. *Gaia*, https://www.gaia.com/video/evidence-our-simulated-reality

Bielawa, Michael J. "Bridgeport's UFO Legacy: Men in Black and the Albert K. Bender Story." Bridgeport History Center. Accessed at: https://bportlibrary.org/hc/authors/bridgeports-ufo-legacy-men-in-black-and-the-albert-k-bender-story/

Fabvssa, Iti. "Spiritual Beliefs and Rituals." *Choctaw Nation of Oklahoma Cultural Services*. Accessed at: http://choctawnationculture.com/media/27420/2009.12%20Spiritual%20beliefs%20and%20rituals.pdf

Guiley, Rosemary Ellen and Imbrogno, Philip J. *The Vengeful Djinn: Unveiling The Hidden Agendas Of Genies*. Woodbury, Minnesota, Llewellyn Publications, 2011.

Hancock, Graham. *America Before: The Key To Earth's Lost Civilization*. New York, New York: St. Martin's Press, 2019.

HealthLine. "Night Terrors." *HealthLine*. Accessed at: https://www.healthline.com/health/night-terrors

HeartMath Institute. *Science of the Heart: Exploring the Role of the Heart in Human Performance*. Accessed at: https://www.heartmath.org/research/science-of-the-heart/energetic-communication/

Holzer, Alexandra. *Growing Up Haunted: A Ghostly Memoir*. Atglen, Pennsylvania: Schiffer Publishing, 2008.

Holzer, Hans. *Murder In Amityville*. New York City, New York: Belmont Tower Books, 1979.

Johnson, Carl L. and Brock, Lana J. *Shadow Realms: Demonology Handbook*. North Charleston, South Carolina, Create Space Independent Publishing Platform, 2017.

Langdon, Stephen Herbert. *The Mythology Of All Races Semitic*. Boston, Massachusetts: Marshall Jones Company, 1931.

Lloyd, Ellen. "Mysterious Hockomock Swamp – A Vortex To The Unknown in Massachusetts?" *AncientPages*. Accessed at: http://www.ancientpages.com/2019/10/09/mysterious-hockomock-swamp-a-vortex-to-the-unknown-in-massachusetts/

Lynn, Heather. *Evil Archaeology: Demons, Possessions, and Sinister Relics*. Newburyport, Massachusetts: Disinformation Books, 2019.

Mark, Joshua J., "Cats In The Ancient World." *Ancient History Encyclopedia.* Accessed at: https://www.ancient.eu/article/466/cats-in-the-ancient-world/

Oleson, Jacob. "Blue Color Meaning – The Color Blue." *Color Meanings*. Accessed at https://www.color-meanings.com/blue-color-meaning-the-color-blue/
"Purple Color Meaning – The Color Purple." *Color Meanings*. Accessed at https://www.color-meanings.com/purple-color-meaning-the-color-purple/
"Yellow Color Meaning – The Color Yellow." *Color Meanings*. Accessed at https://www.color-meanings.com/yellow-color-meaning-the-color-yellow/

Olunu, Esther. "Sleep Paralysis, a Medical Condition with a Diverse Cultural Interpretation." Accessed at https://www.ncbi.nlm.nih.gov/pmc/articles/PMC6082011/

Perron, Andrea. *House Of Darkness House Of Light*. Bloomington, Indiana: Author House, 2011.

ScienceDaily. "Quantum Entanglement." ScienceDaily. Accessed: https://www.sciencedaily.com/terms/quantum_entanglement.htm

Silva, Freddy. *The Divine Blueprint: Temples, Power Places And The Global Plan To Shape The Human Soul*. Portland, Maine: Invisible Temple, 2016.

Vehovec, Doug. "Historic sites: Rumors of haunting persist at Madison Seminary. *The News-Herald.* Accessed at: https://www.news-herald.com/news/ohio/historic-sites-rumors-of-haunting-persist-at-madison-seminary/article_6b4fbdc9-aea6-5f1a-95e3-d7434df31a94.html.

Index

About The Author

Mike Ricksecker is the author of the Amazon best-selling *A Walk In The Shadows: A Complete Guide To Shadow People* and the historic paranormal books *Ghosts of Maryland, Ghosts and Legends of Oklahoma, Campfire Tales: Midwest, Ghostorian Case Files*, and the *Encounters With The Paranormal* series. He has appeared on multiple television shows and programs as a paranormal historian, including Travel Channel's *The Alaska Triangle*, Discovery+'s *Fright Club*, Animal Planet's *The Haunted*, Bio Channel's *My Ghost Story*, and RenTV's (Russia) *Mysteries of Mankind*. Mike also produces his own Internet supernatural-based shows on the Haunted Road Media YouTube channel, and is the producer and director of the docu-series, *The Shadow Dimension*, available on several streaming platforms.

On Tuesday and Wednesday nights, he hosts *The Edge of the Rabbit Hole* livestream show and the *Connecting the Universe* interactive class, respectively. Haunted Road Media is also his own paranormal and supernatural book publishing and video production company representing a number of paranormal authors, winning the award for Excellent Media In The Paranormal Field at the 2019 Shockfest Film Festival.

Mike's historic paranormal articles have been published in *The Baltimore Sun, Paranormal Underground Magazine*, and he previously wrote an Oklahoma City paranormal column for Examiner.com (2010 – 2014). His work has also been featured in *The Oklahoman, The Frederick News Post*, Marshall University's *The Parthenon*, and Louisiana State University's *Civil War Book Review*. He now hosts many of these articles along with informational videos and learnings courses on the Connected Universe Portal website.

A native of Cleveland, Ohio, Mike is a father of four and is an avid baseball fan.

Other Haunted Road Media titles from Mike Ricksecker:

ALASKA'S MYSTERIOUS TRIANGLE

The Alaska Triangle, much like its counterpart, the Bermuda Triangle, is one of the most enigmatic places on Earth. Since 1988, over 16,000 people have mysteriously gone missing across its landscape, and over the years this region has played host to some of the strangest phenomena ever recorded. What causes this unexplained activity and what ancient mysteries may be hidden in the Last Frontier?

GHOSTORIAN CASE FILES

Crack open the case files of a Ghostorian and venture into the depths of mysterious historic paranormal investigations! Unlock hidden secrets through exhibits of collected supernatural evidence and carefully researched data, connecting dots that have been centuries in the making.

DEADLY HEIRS

Saying Earl Kiddering is rich is like saying Babe Ruth hit a couple of home runs, but saying he's dead is more accurate. A month after the billionaire drowns in his own swimming pool, Earl's great-niece hires private investigator Chase Michael DeBarlo to find Kiddering's missing will while other family members squabble over the fortune. Deadly Heirs explores the loyalties (and disloyalties) of family bonds.

ENCOUNTERS WITH THE PARANORMAL

Almost everyone has a ghost story. Real people. Real stories. Read about haunted houses and vehicles, experiences during paranormal investigations, visits from relatives that have passed on, pets reacting to the paranormal, psychic experiences, and conversations with full-bodied apparitions. ENCOUNTERS WITH THE PARANORMAL reveals personal stories of the supernatural, exploring the realm beyond the veil.

ENCOUNTERS WITH THE PARANORMAL, Vol. 2

In this second volume, read about more haunted houses, visits from relatives who have passed on, messages from pets from the other side, experiences during paranormal investigations, psychic experiences, hauntings by shadow people, including a dedicated section to the historic Goldenrod Showboat. ENCOUNTERS WITH THE PARANORMAL: Volume 2 reveals more personal stories of the supernatural, continuing to explore the realm beyond the veil.

ENCOUNTERS WITH THE PARANORMAL, Vol. 3

In this third volume, read about more haunted houses, supernatural creatures, messages from pets from the other side, haunted history, experiences during paranormal investigations, psychic experiences, and more, including a dedicated section to the historic Mineral Springs Hotel. ENCOUNTERS WITH THE PARANORMAL: VOLUME 3 reveals more personal stories of the supernatural and paranormal, continuing to explore the realm beyond the veil through its contributors.

ENCOUNTERS WITH THE PARANORMAL, Vol. 4

Volume four of the ENCOUNTERS WITH THE PARANORMAL series covers even more haunted houses, supernatural creatures, experiences during paranormal investigations, haunted history, and psychic experiences than any of its predecessors. You are not alone! This offering also includes a dedicated section to the historic Ferry Plantation and its many haunts.

Join us at the Connected Universe Portal:
connecteduniverseportal.com

And on *The Shadow Dimension* at:
shadowdimension.com

Made in the USA
Las Vegas, NV
13 October 2024